'50s

American Magazine Ads. 3

VARIETY

装幀＝大貫伸樹＋伊藤庸一
Book Design＝Shinju Onuki＋Yoichi Ito

'50s American Magazine Ads.3 VARIETY
Copyright © 1987 Graphic-sha Publishing Co., Ltd.
1-9-12 Kudankita, Chiyoda-ku, Tokyo 102, Japan.

Printed in Japan

First Printing, July 1987

New from Motorola

Sleek wrap-around styling. Seven fadeproof color combinations.

Hi-fi in fiber glass!

Richest sounding, most durable portables ever built

Out of this revolutionary duraphonic fiber glass case comes tone quality you'd expect
to hear only from a hi-fi console! Motorola shaped this tough, light, miracle material into an
almost acoustically perfect case. (Notice how even the lid "baffles" and projects the
sound like a bandshell.) Inside you'll find three hi-fi speakers, an automatic
4-speed record changer, and separate bass-treble controls.

The Motorola Calypso (Model 3H24, above) comes in Caribbean Blue or two-tone
Jamaican Sand and Ivory. And you can choose from phonos, radio-phono combinations, and
hi-fi portables—priced low as $79.95!

Looks and carries
like an expensive
overnight case

MOTOROLA
World's Largest Exclusive Electronics Manufacturer

Prices and specifications subject to change without notice.

Seventeen, December 1957

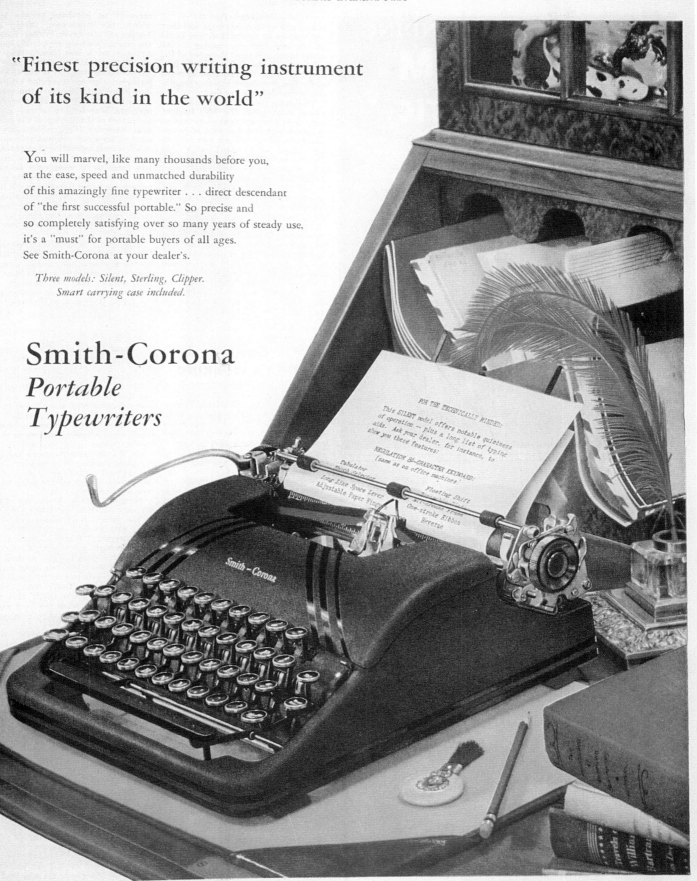

"Finest precision writing instrument of its kind in the world"

You will marvel, like many thousands before you, at the ease, speed and unmatched durability of this amazingly fine typewriter . . . direct descendant of "the first successful portable." So precise and so completely satisfying over so many years of steady use, it's a "must" for portable buyers of all ages. See Smith-Corona at your dealer's.

Three models: Silent, Sterling, Clipper.
Smart carrying case included.

Smith-Corona
Portable Typewriters

L C SMITH & CORONA TYPEWRITERS INC SYRACUSE 1 N Y *Canadian factory and offices, Toronto, Ontario. Makers also of famous Smith-Corona Office Typewriters, Adding Machines, Vivid Duplicators, Ribbons and Carbons*

Saturday Evening Post, January 1950

"Proctor's the gift that says it better!"

says **TERESA WRIGHT**
Starring in "THE MEN"
A Stanley Kramer Production
Released thru United Artists

Best wishes on your wedding day

Happy birthday

Love to mother on her day

Happy anniversary

Whether as a truly thoughtful gift for any occasion or to grace your own table, choose the Proctor Custom Toaster. Proctor is equipped with *exclusive* "Color Guard" —a toast control so accurate it knows whether bread is dry, moist, thick or thin and automatically adjusts the toasting time for each, always providing the color toast you prefer without ever changing the setting. Proctor even reheats toast automatically without burning. No other toaster offers such *extra* performance and *extra* convenience. That is why the Proctor Toaster is the choice of Hollywood stars.
At the best stores everywhere . . . *Price, $22.50**

Special for budgeters. Proctor *Standard* Toaster. Sold a year ago for $18.95 . . . *Now Only $13.95**
Fed. Tax Incl.
PROCTOR ELECTRIC COMPANY, PHILADELPHIA 40, PA.

Beautiful new carton adds charm to Proctor Custom Toaster. Makes your gift more distinctive.

PROCTOR ®

A Joy to have around

HOOVER

MODEL 115

Handiest Cleaner in America...

only **49**⁹⁵

Prices slightly higher in Canada

and your old cleaner

Lady, what a cleaner! Big enough for tough jobs, light enough for quick ones, handy enough to store in "pint-size" space. Model 115 features Hoover's exclusive Triple Action—it beats, as it sweeps, as it cleans—gets the deep-down dirt and keeps colors fresh.

ONLY $5.00 DOWN and easy monthly payments. (Cleaning tools available at slight extra cost.) Hoover Cleaners (three great Triple-Action Cleaners and the new Hoover AERO-DYNE Tank Cleaner) are sold only by established local retail merchants. Look in your classified phone book for the name of your nearest Hoover dealer, and call him *now* for a home showing of this great Hoover value. No obligation, of course.

THE HOOVER COMPANY
North Canton, Ohio; Hamilton, Ontario, Canada; Perivale, England

Prices subject to increase without notice

It Beats as it Sweeps as it Cleans

HOOVER

It beats...
as it sweeps...
as it cleans

You'll be happier with a Hoover

71

Say it with flavors

The candy with the hole ...still only 5¢

Everybody's favorite gobblin'

Your best bet for the
Trick-or-Treat set this Halloween

8...count 'em...8 delicious flavors
the original tasty-thin sugar wafer candy

...and this new Necco treat does the trick, too!

A big double bar of delightful
honeycombed molasses crunch,
spun through and through with
creamy peanut butter...

Necco OK DOUBLE BAR MILK CHOCOLATE PEANUT CRUNCH

...and covered with the
smoothest milk chocolate
you ever tasted.

New England Confectionery Co., Cambridge 39, Mass.

"IT'S A HEART AND DART PARTY I've got cases and cases of COKE"

There's a bright idea at the heart of every great party . . . and a plan that includes Coca-Cola, of course. Our idea: give a dishpan a gaily-colored coat of paint (water-based so it washes off), then decorate with paste-on hearts. And there you are—with the Coke ice-cold and ready when the party starts. The good taste of Coke tells your friends they're specially welcome . . . and its cheerful lift really keeps the party going.

SIGN OF GOOD TASTE

So good in taste, in such good taste

Coca-Cola

Do it yourself with *Light* refreshment

TODAY'S active people do a lot of fixing, but there's little need for them to remodel themselves. Their taste for lighter, less-filling food and drink makes it easy to keep slim and trim.

Pepsi-Cola fits right in with their sensible, modern preference in diet. Today's Pepsi, reduced in calories, is never heavy, never too sweet. Refresh without filling. Have a Pepsi!

Pepsi-Cola refreshes without filling

SEE "CINDERELLA" LIVE IN COLOR
AND BLACK-AND-WHITE ON CBS-TELEVISION, MARCH 31.

Saturday Evening Post, March 1957

You can light either end!

GET SATISFYING FLAVOR...

So _friendly_ to your taste!

See how
Pall Mall's greater length
filters the smoke and
makes it mild—but
does not filter out that
satisfying flavor!

FOR FLAVOR AND MILDNESS, FINE TOBACCO FILTERS BEST

1 You get greater length of the finest tobaccos money can buy **2** Pall Mall's greater length filters the smoke _naturally_... **3** Filters it over, under, around and through Pall Mall's fine tobaccos!

OUTSTANDING... AND THEY ARE MILD!

Product of _The American Tobacco Company_ — "_Tobacco is our middle name_"

Know-how... not say so...
makes **Old Gold**
"the Treasure
of them All"

Old Gold
CIGARETTES

Made by Lorillard, a famous name
in tobacco for nearly 200 years

For a Treat instead of a Treatment... treat yourself to **OLD GOLDS**

"World Series U. S. A.," by John Falter.   Number 86 in the series "Home Life in America"

In this friendly, freedom-loving land of ours—Beer belongs...enjoy it!

BEER AND ALE—AMERICA'S BEVERAGES OF MODERATION
Sponsored by the United States Brewers Foundation...Chartered 1862

For
perfect
days

For perfect days—no other month like June. For perfect
drinks—no other whiskey like Seagram's 7 Crown. Its
magnificent taste makes even a June day *more perfect*.

Say **Seagram's** *and be* **Sure**

SEAGRAM'S 7 CROWN. **Blended Whiskey.** 86.8 PROOF. 65% GRAIN NEUTRAL SPIRITS. SEAGRAM-DISTILLERS CORPORATION, CHRYSLER BUILDING, NEW YORK

'50s

雑誌広告にみるアメリカングラフィティ
ザ・フィフティーズ
3

バラエティ

アメリカでは「広告は社会を映す鏡である」といわれる。そして，その鏡（ミラー）を作る人たちということで，広告制作者のことを“ミラー・メーカーズ”などと呼ぶそうである。

　では，広告という“鏡”に映し出されたアメリカの’50年代はどんな時代だったのか，’50年代を広告を通してみてみようではないか，という発想が具体化して本書ができた。

　ライフ (Life)，サタデー・イブニング・ポスト (The Saturday Evening Post)，コリアーズ (Collier's)，ルック (Look)，ホリデー (Holiday) といった’50年代に全盛期にあった大型グラフ雑誌に載った商品広告や企業広告のなかから選び出した“優秀作品”で構成したものが本書である。

　第1巻が「クルマ」(Automobile)，第2巻が「ファッション」(Fashion Apparel)，第3巻が「バラエティ」(Variety) という3巻組みになっていて，本巻はその第3巻である。

　「バラエティ」というのは，いろいろな物の取り合わせ，ちょっと悪い言い方をすれば寄せ集めという意味だが，たしかに家電製品，音響機器，オフィス用品，食品，酒類，清涼飲料，煙草，公共サービス，航空などと多種多様の広告が収録してある。

　では，本題にもどって，それらバラエティに富む広告という鏡が映し出したアメリカの’50年代とは一体どんな時代だったのだろうか。ひとつひとつの広告を丹念に見ていくと，どの広告にも共通して，一種独特な天真爛漫な明るさがあることに気付かれると思う。広告のなかに描かれている人物の表情も底抜けに明るい。このイノセントな明るさこそが“ザ・フィフティーズ”感覚だ。

'50年代のアメリカは，まことに明るい，楽天主義が充満している
ような国だった。第2次大戦の戦勝国として，世界一の超大国にの
し上った自信からくる高揚した国家意識と，史上まれにみる戦後の
好景気のなかで，アメリカの'50年代はまさしくバラ色であった。

　当然のこととして，企業の広告活動も活発で，広告費は10年間で
2倍になり，各メディアには広告やCMが溢れんばかりであった。
広告コピーには，「輝かしいアメリカ」「楽しいアメリカ」「豊かなア
メリカ」が謳われ，アメリカ人の多くが素直にそれを信じた。'50年
代はそんな時代であった。

　公害も，嫌煙権も，省エネルギーも，貿易赤字も，失業も，まし
てエイズも存在しなかった，古き良き時代だった。そして，なによ
りアメリカを明るくしていたのは，深刻な人種問題がなかったことだ
ろう。なかったというより，未だ表面化していなかったといってもよい。

　多くの読者諸氏はすぐに気付かれるだろうが，'50年代の広告には，
黒人や少数民族はほとんど登場しない。モデルは徹底して白人，そ
れもアングロサクソン系が使われた。いわゆる*WASP*（白人で，アングロサクソンで，プロテスタント）の価値観が
絶対視され，黒人や少数民族のそれは頭から否定され，排除されたのである。
'50年代のアメリカは100パーセント白人国家だったのである。

　'50年代の広告を特徴づける第3の点は，広告手法にあるといえる。
'50年代は商品自体をどーんと真正面から押し出すという直接的なや
り方は好まれなかった。白人中流家庭の日常生活の一場面を描いて，
そのなかにさりげなく商品を配するといったような手法がとられた。
広告の主題はいつも"アメリカン・ウエイ・オブ・リビング"であ
った。だから，そこには当時の流行や風俗やアメリカ人の夢，アメ
リカン・ドリームそのものが描かれたのである。

さらに，'50年代の広告に表われた変化のひとつは，前面に若者が
登場してきたことだった。それもティーンズと呼ばれる13歳から19歳までのヤングである。

　「ティーンズこそ最高の顧客である。アメリカのティーン・エイジ
ャーの女の子だけが使うお金は1年間42.5億ドルを超す。男の子の
分を含めれば100億ドルに近づくだろう。しかもこれには大人なら
ば当然支払わなければならない税金や保険料や家賃や光熱費などは
まったく含まれていない。純粋に消費のためのお金である」セブンティーン誌はこう書いた。
　"ヤングを狙え"というのが，各企業の合い言葉になり，ユース・
マーケットという新語が生まれたのも'50年代半ばのことである。若
者だけをターゲットにした広告キャンペーンが盛んになり，市場のセグメンテーションが
急速に進んだ。

　さらにもう一点，'50年代の広告を特徴づけている事実がある。そ
れは'50年代まで，最大の広告媒体は雑誌だったということである。
なかでも本書に収録した広告の"取材源"となった大型グラフ雑誌は，メジャー中のメジャーな広告メディア
であった。

　'50年代の初期にはじまった全米テレビ放送は，急成長を遂げつつ
あったが，未だメジャーではなかった。全米をカバーする信頼でき
る広告媒体はナショナル・マガジンのみであった。（'60年代に入る
と，各メディア間の地位が逆転する。大スポンサーの関心はテレビ
に向かい，雑誌に対する広告出稿量も減少の一途をたどる。そして
'60年代後半から'70年代にかけて，大型グラフ雑誌はいずれも相次いで廃刊に追い込まれる
のである。）

本書に収録したような大型で，しかもバラエティに富む広告が大
量に，毎号の雑誌に掲載されたのは'50年代までのことであった。あらましこんなことが'50年代の雑誌広告の背景である。

　'50年代からすでに30数年が経ったいま，これら古き良き時代の広
告を眺めていると，陽炎の底から浮かび出るように，ザ・フィフテ
ィーズの情景のひとつ，ひとつが想い出される。'50年代のアメリカ
は何故にこうも強く私たちをひきつけるのだろうか。理由はいろい
ろ考えられる。しかし，なんといっても，私たちが'50年代のアメリ
カに惹かれる最大の理由は，現在の私たちのライフ・スタイルそのものの原点がそこにあるからではないか，
と私は思う。

　私たちが信奉しているデモクラシーの精神も，ウェイ・オブ・ラ
イフも，そして多分に物質主義優先の価値観も，なにもかもが，'50
年代のアメリカに学び，教わったものだからではないだろうか。'50
年代のアメリカをみるとき，私たちは自らの原点と，若く，希望に
満ちていた頃の自らの青春の姿をそこにみて，胸を熱くするのである。

　最後に，本書の制作にあたっては，ブックデザインを担当して下
さった大貫伸樹氏とその事務所の皆さん，ならびに版元であるグラ
フィック社編集部の山田信彦氏に心からの感謝の意をあらわしたい。
　これらの人々の激励とご協力によって，私は8カ月間に及ぶ制作
期間中を通じて，つねにザ・フィフティーズへのノスタルジーに浸
りながら，まことに心愉しい作業をつづけることができたのである。

編者　生田保年

In America, advertizing is said to be the 'ever-present mirror of society', and thus those who create the advertizing might be called the 'mirror-makers'.

But what was reflected in the advertizing 'looking glass' of the nineteen-fifties? This book is a full retrospective of the period, an answer to this question through a visual study of the advertizing of the times.

The large format text and picture weeklies that flourished in this golden age——Life, The Saturday Evening Post, Collier's, Look, Holiday——are the sources for the superb examples of merchandise and corporate advertizing that make up 'Variety'. This is the third and final edition of the series, following 'Automobiles' and 'Fashion Apparel'.

As the title suggests, advertisements for various amenities have been included in these pages, such as appliances, hi-fi equipment, office machines, food, liquor, beverages, cigarettes, airlines and many others. But to return to the original question, what was the world reflected in the wealth of advertizing that has been gathered here into the category 'Variety'?

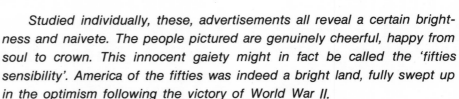

Studied individually, these, advertisements all reveal a certain brightness and naivete. The people pictured are genuinely cheerful, happy from soul to crown. This innocent gaiety might in fact be called the 'fifties sensibility'. America of the fifties was indeed a bright land, fully swept up in the optimism following the victory of World War II.

Rising suddenly to the position of the most powerful country in the world, while at the same time enjoying historically unprecedented economic prosperity, Americans experienced an enhanced sense of pride and nationhood that is hardly surprising. A rosier picture can hardly be imagined.

Business activity and economic growth led to a doubling in advertizing outlays by the end of the decade, when virtually every media was brimming with commercials and advertisements. The copy of the times read 'sparkling America' 'pleasant America' or 'rich America' and for the most part people were happy to believe in all this.

And there was no pollution in those days, no anti-smoking campaigns, energy shortages, trade deficits or unemployment, to say nothing of a scourge like the acquired immune deficiency syndrome. Those were indeed the good ol' days.

And what contributed perhaps more significantly to American's lightheartedness was the absence of any acknowledged human rights problems. These issues as yet remained below the surface of society.

As many readers will be quick to notice, there are no blacks or other minority races appearing in the advertisements of this period. The models are without exception white, all falling neatly into the category which was sometime later to be labeled WASP. Everything was designed to appeal to this group's values and tastes, as if they were the only ones which existed. America of the fifties was in one respect homogenous, a white nation.

Another distinction regarding the advertizing of the fifties concerns technique. The practice of pushing the advertized object nakedly to the front was unpopular in those days. Rather, it was preferred to display goods in an inconspicuous manner, surrounded by people relaxing in a typical, middle-class American setting. The underlying theme was always the

'American way of life'. Every effort was made to realize the essential flavor and vision of America, to promote as clearly as possible the American dream.

Another novel development in the advertizing of the fifties was the introduction of young people to the forefront of the advertisements. According to an issue of Seventeen magazine, 'Teenagers are the most important of all customers. Teenage American girls alone spend over four billion dollars a year, and if the amount boys spend is added the amount easily nears ten billion. Naturally the payments parents must make on housing costs, energy bills, taxes, insurance and what have you are in no way included in this figure. This is money spent purely on consumer items.'

'Aim young' became the marketing man's pasword in the fifties, and the concept of a youth market took hold during the middle of the period. Advertizing campaigns targeting the younger generation became prevalent, and in little time the segmentation of marketing became a reality.

But above all it must be remembered that the text and picture weeklies were, through the fifties, the reigning medium of advertisement. The works collected in this book were all taken from the dominant publications of the most powerful advertizing medium of the age. Television had been around since the early fifties, and its growth was swift, but it did not reach comparable dimensions until later. Magazines remained the almighty advertizing source of the fifties. (In the sixties, however, the two positions were reversed. Major sponsors began looking to television, and magazines fell into an inevitable and irreversible decline. From the middle of the sixties through to the early seventies the popular weeklies were shut down and abandoned, one after another.)

The unique style of rich, large-format variety advertizing which this book contains was a phenomenon of the fifties weekly, a medium which saturated the country from coast to coast. Thirty years have elapsed since the fifties, but looking over the pages of this book one certainly senses again the atmosphere those years. It shines warmly, rising up golden from the pages, calling up in our minds old images and memories, working a strange and powerful charm on us.

Several reasons for this attraction can be imagined, but by far the greatest, I believe, is the feeling we have that the roots of our own modern lifestyle are to be found there. Our faith in the spirit of democracy and our materialistic values, things we learned from fifties America, are likewise ideas to be considered. Then again, though, when we look back at the fifties we see ourselves in our youth, when we were filled with hopes and aspirations, and something warms inside of us.

In conclusion, regarding the production of the book, I wish to express my sincerest thanks to Shinju Onuki and those in his office who helped him with the design of the book, and then to Nobuhiko Yamada of Graphic-sha's editorial staff, for his invaluable work. Owing to the generous cooperation of these individuals I have experienced in the past eight months of work not only nostalgia for the fifties, but more importantly, pleasure to the very finish.

Yasutoshi Ikuta

A Note on this Book

The editor and publisher gratefully acknowledge
the invaluable help of all those who contributed to
the compilation of this book.
Especially they express their appreciation to the
advertisers who have generously had their advertisements
reproduced here.

Advertisement Size : Most of the advertisements
reproduced in this book have been reduced in size
on account of the design of the book.

All advertisements, except as otherwise credited,
come from the files of Yasutoshi Ikuta's private
collection of magazine advertisement.

CAMERAS!
cameras!
CAMERAS!

...that say Merry Merry Christmas!

Argus 75 . . . *the easiest of all cameras to use!* It has a big view-finder—a simple, synchronized plug-in flash (to take indoor or dark-day pictures). For the photographer who wants good black and white or color pictures the *easy* way, *it's ideal!* Camera only **$15.95.***

Argus C3 . . . *America's most popular 35 mm camera!* It has everything any photographer would want: a Cintar f:3.5 coated lens; a gear-controlled shutter with speeds up to 1/300 second; a synchronized flash attachment; a split-field range finder! Only **$69.50*** complete with carrying case and flash unit!

Argus C4 . . . *Newest, finest 35 mm camera of them all!* With Super-fast, Cintar f:2.8 lens; most accurate shutter mechanism built, with speeds of 1/10 to 1/200 second; synchronized flash that permits the use of *all* types of bulbs at *all* shutter speeds. Only **$99.50.***

Argus 40 . . . *a brilliant reflex camera—for beginners or experts!* Its bright view-finder —its plug-in flash unit—its 1/25 to 1/150 shutter makes it a wonderful all-time, all-around camera buy! Camera only **$39.95.***

Argus P BB 200 . . . *the world's finest home slide projector!* It has the best optical system made . . . it delivers more light—better illumination . . . its quiet blower keeps it cool—protects your valuable color slides—always! A perfect gift for any photographer! Only **$44.95.***

Argus Gift Box . . . It includes the popular ARGUS 75 camera, leather carrying case, plug-in flash unit, batteries, flash lamps and film . . . everything it takes to make good pictures! Ask your ARGUS dealer about it!

argus

—the world's largest manufacturer of 35 mm. cameras

© Argus Cameras, Inc., Ann Arbor, Michigan

*Prices include Federal Excise Tax and are subject to change without notice.

Saturday Evening Post, December 1951

25

New Zenith "TRANS-OCEANIC"

Here's the new edition of the world-famous portable that out-performs any other, any time, anywhere! It's an even more powerful, more sensitive "TRANS-OCEANIC." Yet it's lighter, easier to carry, and has a new low price tag! Plays where ordinary portables won't—in boats, trains, planes, remote areas. Exclusive Wavemagnet† and Waverod bring in Standard Broadcast, plus international Short Wave on 5 separate bands. "Tropic-Treated" against humidity, radio's deadliest enemy. Works on thrifty, long-life battery, and on AC or DC.

Only $99⁹⁵*
Less Batteries

New Zenith "*Tip-Top* HOLIDAY"†

Swing the lid up—there's the giant "Tip-Top" Dial, actually *above* the set for tip-top tuning ease. Wavemagnet inside lid also tips up, *doubles* the sensitivity of this amazing portable! Open lid, set's on—close lid, set's off! Special Outdoor Tone Circuit gives rich, full tone even in wide open spaces. Works on battery, AC or DC. Handsome cabinet in gleaming black or two tone blue-grey plastic.

Only $39⁹⁵*
Less Batteries

Get ready to rave—
Here's the Parade of New Zenith Portables!

Exciting new values that only Zenith†, world's leader in portable radios, could bring you. See them at your Zenith dealer's now!

New "ZENETTE"† by Zenith

Tiny and exquisite as a jewel, yet a giant in power and volume! Has the biggest speaker Zenith has ever used in a set this size. Lift lid, set's playing—shut lid, set's off! Built-in Wavemagnet for extra sensitivity. Plays on battery, AC or DC. Weighs a mere 5½ lbs. Ultra-smart plastic case in maroon, jet black or white.

Only $39⁹⁵*
Less Batteries

ZENITH
•LONG DISTANCE• RADIO and TELEVISION
THE ROYALTY OF RADIO AND TELEVISION

Zenith "POP-OPEN" Universal†

Fun's a-popping for sure, when you play this sensational Zenith performer. Just press the Pop-Open Button, and everything happens at once! Doors pop open, Wavemagnet pops up, set starts playing! Super-Size speaker gives remarkable volume and tone richness. Operates on battery, AC or DC. Stunning black and silver or two tone grey-beige plastic cabinet.

Only $59⁷⁰*
Less Batteries

*West Coast prices slightly higher. Prices subject to change without notice.

†® ©1949   Over 30 Years of "Know-How" in Radionics† Exclusively   ZENITH RADIO CORPORATION, CHICAGO 39, ILL. • Also Makers of America's Finest Hearing Aids

Holiday, October 1949

Brownie Hawkeye Camera, Flash Model—
$7.45 It's the slickest "Brownie" that
Kodak has ever made. Gets grand snaps
with traditional "Brownie" press-the-button
ease. Flasholder with guard, $3.95. Complete
gift kit—camera, Flasholder, film, flash
lamps, batteries, 2 helpful booklets—$13.75.

Kodak Pony 828 Camera—$32 Gets
sparkling color slides for projection or
prints. Flasholder with guard, $12.35.
Complete gift kit—camera, field case,
Flasholder, black-and-white and full-color
film, flash lamps, batteries—$55.

Kodak Duaflex II Camera, Kodet Lens—
$14.95 Big, hooded view finder lets you see
your picture before you shoot. De luxe model
with Kodar *f*/8 Lens, $22.95. Flasholder with
guard, $3.50. Complete gift kit—camera with
f/8 lens, Flasholder, film, flash lamps, batteries,
2 helpful booklets—$29.25.

A Kodak camera is 3 exciting gifts in 1

1 It's a black-and-white camera

2 It's a color camera

3 It's a "flash" camera

. . . That's why it's so satisfying to *give* a Kodak camera. It's
such an accomplished gift . . . an important personal possession
bringing immediate and lasting pleasure to young and old.

You'll find Kodak cameras in a wide range of models and
prices. Why not start shopping on this page, and continue at
your dealer's? This Christmas, you'll make someone's home
a happy home indeed—if you give a Kodak camera.

Eastman Kodak Company, Rochester 4, N. Y.

Kodak Tourist II Camera, Kodet Lens—$27 Up to
the minute in style, simplicity, versatility—it's Kodak's
famous folding camera. Other models to $100.
Flasholder with guard, $12.35.

Brownie Movie Camera—only $44.50 Loads and
shoots as easily as a box "Brownie." F/2.7 lens gets
crisp, clear 8mm. movies in color or black-and-white
. . . and with an inexpensive flood lamp or two,
gets them indoors as well as out.

Kodak
TRADE-MARK

Prices are subject to change without notice and include Federal Tax applicable when this advertisement was released for publication.

Saturday Evening Post, September 1958

only 2 simple controls

TURN IT ON 🔘 – 🔘 SELECT STATION – that's all!

BRAND-NEW and BEAUTIFUL CONSOLE gives life-size pictures at lower cost!

BILT-IN-TENNA
No outside antenna in good signal areas.

16" BROADVIEW SCREEN
Life-size pictures of startling new clarity.

Want your TV BIG? Want it BRIGHTER and CLEARER than ever before? Want it in a BEAUTIFUL mahogany or limed oak cabinet? Then ask your dealer for a demonstration of the new Motorola 16K2. It's one of a *brand new* line of magnificent Motorola's—more handsome—better performing and yes, LOWER PRICED—8½ to 19½ inch screen sizes—to fit every home and budget. *See them soon!*

See your classified directory for your nearest Motorola dealer.

Motorola TELEVISION

WILLIAM BOYD as HOPALONG CASSIDY America's favorite Television Cowboy

Life, April 1951

29

Look at the new Motorola Portables!

The handle is a rotating antenna

You just turn the handle (not the radio) for stronger, clearer reception. Because it's three times as big as other portable antennas, and turns to face signals head-on, you bring in stations you've never heard before on a portable. Sets use AC, DC current or batteries. Shatterproof steel cabinets are covered with scuffproof, stain-resistant miracle fabric.

See them—*hear them*—at your Motorola dealer.

CITATION — comes in charcoal, green, red or blue, with clear plastic and gold front. $34.95*

SPECTATOR—Taupe color case, with chocolate brown plastic trim. Exclusive Roto-tenna handle. Only $29.95*

DIPLOMAT — The extra-long-range 6-tube portable. Ebony or suntan, gold-finished trim. $59.95*

PIXIE — World's most powerful pocket radio. Twice the power—twice the battery life, too. Motorola Golden Voice. Only $29.95 in suntan or ebony, earphone jack. (Carrying case available at slight extra cost.)

CARIBBEAN — Deluxe gold-trimmed design, in white or suntan color, chocolate brown Roto-tenna handle; or charcoal with ebony handle. $39.95

Motorola, Inc., WORLD'S LARGEST EXCLUSIVE ELECTRONICS MANUFACTURER

*Prices slightly higher in South and West. Batteries extra for all. Prices and specifications subject to change without notice.

TAKE IT
EVERYWHERE
EXCEPT TO
CLASSES!

ZENITH
Musical Roommate

Zenith Portable Cobra-Matic® Phono-graph. Opens full 90° for easy record loading. Washable, wear-resistant blue Pyroxylin finish. Model S9013. $99.95*

Heading back to school? Better take Zenith this semester. Here's a Zenith portable phonograph you can take to house parties and dances, too. Has a specially mounted changer and tone arm hold, for moving about without damage. Side-mounted volume and tone controls operate with top down. Convenient carrying handle. Smart as the smartest luggage.

 And what music it makes! ZENITH COBRA-MATIC RECORD PLAYER plays not only 78, 45, 33⅓ and the new 16⅔ RPM talking book speed... but any speed from 10 to 85 RPM! Fully variable speed regulator lets you adjust turntable for exact recorded pitch and tempo. Or you can change key for singing, speed up or slow down tempo for dancing! Automatically changes stacks of 10 records.

Lightweight Zenith Cobra® Tone Arm makes records sound better, last longer. 7½-inch Zenith-built Speaker has Alnico 5 magnet for rich, vibrant basses and beautifully clear trebles.

See it—and see other smart Zenith phonographs, radios and combinations at your Zenith Dealer's now.

 **Zenith Cobra-Matic Record Player with Stroboscope.** Dots of light show when records play at exact speeds, for perfect pitch and tempo. Full-toned. Brush-wood finish cabinet. Model S9012, $79.95*. Without Stroboscope, Model S9011, $69.95*

ZENITH
The royalty of television and RADIO

ALSO MAKERS OF FINE HEARING AIDS
Zenith Radio Corporation · Chicago 39, Illinois

*Manufacturer's suggested re-tail price, slightly higher in Far West and South. Specifications subject to change.

You shall have music wherever you go!

Made for play at home or away you'll find that good times, good friends, gaiety, just naturally tag along with the melodious tone of a V-M portable phonograph. So light, so easy to carry, you'll take it with you wherever you go.

V-M Model 556 Portable High Fidelity Phonograph has all the new features you want, many are exclusive with V-M. There's the brand new V-M tone-o-matic® that lets you simultaneously balance both bass and treble tones to the degree you desire in authentic high fidelity response. Power control regulates this predetermined response to provide the power level most suitable for your listening comfort. Speaker system includes two extended-range tweet-er-woofer speakers for superb richness in tonal quality. Built-in receptacle allows you to play your AM-FM radio or TV tuner through the magnificent speaker amplifier system. Scuff- and water-resistant leatherette case in choice of Rose and Gray or rich brown. Powerful 5-watt amplifier plus many other outstanding features make this a truly re-markable value at $119.95.

Voice of Music Model 990 is the world's *smallest, lightest* automatic, three-speed portable phonograph! Big folded horn speaker in the lid thrills you with rich-toned console-quality music from a compact, easy-to-carry instrument. Free-floating tone arm has dual sapphire needles in a new, all-weather ceramic cartridge. Beautiful rose and gray leatherette case. $69.95.*

Slightly higher in the west

UL Approved

the Voice of Music

V-M CORPORATION, BENTON HARBOR, MICHIGAN
WORLD'S LARGEST MANUFACTURER OF PHONOGRAPHS AND RECORD CHANGERS

women dreamed them...home economists planned them...

SEE THE NEW PANTRY-DOR FOR HANDY STORAGE
plus these features in the big 9.2 cu. ft. model

✓ tapered *"Shadowline"* styling saves space in your kitchen

✓ *bottle opener* always handy; built-in on door frame—exclusive!

✓ huge full-width *freezer locker* for 50 pounds of frozen food

✓ *"Diffuse-O-Lite"* illuminates entire interior—exclusive!

✓ *cold from top to bottom* for safe, tested refrigeration; stainless steel shelves

✓ full width crisper *and* extra crisper hold fully 23.3 quarts

INTERNATIONAL HARVESTER

"Here's the roomy G·E Refrigerator my family won't outgrow!"

Here's a new and wonderful refrigerator in which there's room for everything . . . *and everything can be kept in its proper place at the proper temperature.* It's ONE refrigerator your family won't outgrow!

Furthermore, this G-E Refrigerator-Food Freezer Combination occupies no more floor space than old-style refrigerators.

Truly, it's General Electric's finest and most efficient refrigerator in 25 years. Your G-E dealer will be glad to show it to you. Look for his name in the classified section of your telephone directory. General Electric Company, Louisville 2, Kentucky.

TRADE NOW

Trade in your old refrigerator *now.* Get a new G-E Refrigerator-Freezer, actually *two* great appliances in one smart new cabinet!

For a limited time, G-E dealers are offering very special trade-in allowances on old refrigerators—*regardless of make.* Chances are such an allowance will cover the entire down payment.

So why not take advantage of this opportunity? During hot weather many an old refrigerator doesn't protect food properly, yet uses over twice the current of a new G-E! Trade *now!*

Foods stay crisp, fresh! *Frost does not* build up in fresh-food section. Uncovered foods do not dry out.

Keeps a full pound of butter at just the right temperature for easy mixing and spreading.

This new *Space Maker* Door has thick aluminum shelves that are so *deep,* so *wide,* and so *sturdy!*

For 25 years G. E. has pioneered most of the great developments in mechanical refrigeration.

So dependable! More than 3,500,000 in use 10 years or longer!

GENERAL ⊕ ELECTRIC

Only the *Sunbeam*
toasts with RADIANT CONTROL
Automatic Beyond Belief!

All you do is drop in the bread

Bread lowers itself automatically, no levers to push

Toast raises itself silently, without popping or banging

THIS is the entirely *new* toaster that has completely changed people's conception of what an automatic toaster should do! Only after you've seen it make toast can you appreciate the sheer magic of its care-free operation.

No levers to push—no popping or banging. Just drop in the bread and let the Sunbeam take over. The bread lowers itself, turning on the current. When perfectly toasted, the toast comes up silently, and current turns off. It's *that* sensational.

The new Sunbeam even regulates the toasting *automatically*, depending on the *kind* of bread. If the slices are moist, it toasts them a little longer than if they are dry. If they are thin, it toasts them quicker than thicker slices. Moist or dry, thick or thin— you always get the same uniform golden color you want—*automatically*. There is no other automatic toaster like the Sunbeam because only the Sunbeam toasts with patented RADIANT CONTROL. Ask your Sunbeam dealer to demonstrate it for you.

© SUNBEAM CORPORATION, Dept. 53 Chicago 50, Illinois • Toronto 9, Canada

Give Sunbeam and you give the finest

Automatically adjusts itself for every kind of bread
—moist or dry, thick slices or thin

The heat radiated from the *actual surface of the bread* is focused on a sensitive strip of bimetal. When the bread reaches the scientifically correct temperature for perfect toasting, sufficient heat is absorbed by the thermostat to shut off the toaster. The toasting is always the same no matter what kind of bread you use, regardless of line voltage, once you set it for the brownness you want.

Only Sunbeam has patented
RADIANT CONTROL

Happy the Hostess
that Santa favors
with this Hospitality Set!

ON WITH THE NEW!
On with many a new year of *confident* home entertaining. Makes the simplest foods so inviting —the most unexpected guest so easy to serve.

TELEVISION'S TWIN!
Smart snack service— *while the show is on!* This new "Hospitality"* Set gives the *hostess* time for fun. She'll bless you!

$32.50
Set includes toaster, tray, four party plates, and three relish dishes.
Toaster only, $21.50

Look for the TOASTMASTER Name on Your Toaster... Others Will!

The New
TOASTMASTER
Hospitality Set

GRAND SLAM
in happier hostessing! The four party plates of Viking crystal glassware lend real festivity to the most informal affair.

NO GUESSING-GAME!
Everyone *knows* the "Toastmaster"* Toaster. For entertaining, or at the family table —it's America's *most-wanted* toaster.

GIVE HER TIME FOR TALK
Handsome, walnut-veneer tray inlaid with simulated leather invites guests to serve themselves —and have fun doing it.

*"TOASTMASTER" and "HOSPITALITY" are registered trademarks of McGraw Electric Company, makers of "Toastmaster" Toasters, "Toastmaster" Electric Water Heaters, and other "Toastmaster" Products. Copyright 1949, TOASTMASTER PRODUCTS DIVISION, McGraw Electric Company, Elgin, Ill.

Saturday Evening Post, December 1950

NO DUST BAG TO EMPTY

APPROVED BY UNDERWRITERS LABORATORIES

The world's most modern Vacuum Cleaner

VACUUM **LEWYT** CLEANER

Guaranteed by Good Housekeeping

no muss...no fuss DO IT with LEWYT

NO MUSS! NO FUSS! NO DUST BAG! Nothing to shake out! The bag's *gone*, the bother's *gone*! Lewyt's metal Dust Bowl empties *clean* in seconds!

NO LEAKING DUST! Only Lewyt filters dust 4 ways—gives you "hospital clean" air to breathe! Allergy sufferers love their Lewyts!

NEW MAGIC "ENERGIZER"! Automatically maintains peak cleaning power. Dirt can't choke-off suction as with conventional cleaners!

SPECIAL DUSTING BRUSH! Whisks away dirt from venetian blinds, furniture, books, lamps—does *all* your dusting!

SWEEPS BARE FLOORS . . . brightens draperies and upholstery . . . cleans radiators . . . even de-moths your closets!

NO TELEVISION INTERFERENCE! Lewyt's exclusive "Video-pak" prevents distortion of radio and television reception!

SPRAYS PAINT! New professional-type Spray-gun saves you time and effort! Lewyt waxes linoleum, too!

LIGHT, EASY TO USE! Easy to store! *Everything*, including new Lock-seal tubes, tucks neatly away!

IT'S QUIET—NO ROAR!
Lewyt is *super-powerful*, yet truly *super-quiet*. You can even clean the nursery without waking the baby!

PRESERVES YOUR RUGS!
New No. 80 Carpet Nozzle gets more embedded dirt...picks up more lint, threads, dog hairs...all with *less rug wear!*

10 HANDY ATTACHMENTS!
No extras to buy! Complete with all cleaning tools, Lewyt is actually priced *below* many old-fashioned cleaners!

LEWYT COSTS NO MORE THAN ORDINARY CLEANERS!

Ask your Lewyt Dealer for free Home Demonstration. See your Classified Telephone Directory.

LARGER MODELS NOW AVAILABLE FOR HOSPITALS, HOTELS, CLUBS, THEATRES, OFFICES, INSTITUTIONS!

Write for details!

FREE PICTURE BOOKLET ON MODERN HOME CLEANING!

LEWYT CORPORATION, Vacuum Cleaner Div. Dept. 4, 70 Broadway, Brooklyn 11, New York

Without obligation, rush me FREE copy of Lewyt's Picture Booklet on Modern Home Cleaning!

NAME..

ADDRESS..

CITY..

COUNTY..................................STATE.................

5

No stretching for high places. Handy, light tools.

The right tool for every purpose. You stay fresh —your room comes clean.

Just a "click" and you're all ready for above-the-floor cleaning.

Exclusive! The famous Hoover Triple-Action principle. It beats, as it sweeps, as it cleans.* No trick to pick up dog hairs, lint, pesky surface litter.

TRIPLE ACTION. It stands up to you. Just guide it; see how easily it rolls. Hoover's gentle-but-thorough Triple Action gets deep-down dirt, keeps rug colors bright. Prolongs rug life. It beats . . . as it sweeps . . . as it cleans.* Model 28, cleaner alone **$69⁹⁵**

Cleaning tools in neat, easy-to-carry kit **$18⁰⁰**

Choose the type of cleaner you want— with the name most women prefer

HOOVER

Of course you want a Hoover Cleaner— most women do, 2 to 1 over any other make. But which type? The famous Triple-Action Hoover or the new Hoover Cylinder Cleaner? See and try both at your dealer's now. Then choose.

THE HOOVER COMPANY
North Canton, Ohio • Hamilton, Ontario, Canada

TRIPLE-ACTION
MODEL 28

CYLINDER
MODEL 50

CYLINDER. Cleans by powerful suction. No stooping to attach or detach hose. New idea in dirt disposal—the Dirt Ejector. Your hands never touch dirt or bag. Quick, simple, clean! Stores in small space. Non-marking skids. Most convenient cleaner of its type. Model 50, complete with tools in light, handy kit, Mothimizer and sprayer . . **$79⁵⁰**

Slides easily under cabinets, sofas, chairs and other heavy furniture.

No stooping to attach or detach hose. Just touch toe release.

Dirt Ejector— just flick toe release. Dirt shakes out.

No reaching with Hoover's smart, light extension tools.

a Magic Chef double feature

GREATEST *Magic Chef* YET! IT'S AUTOMATIC

two big ovens—one for baking and roasting—one for broiling, barbecuing, food warming

FOR THE FIRST TIME!
A Range of individuality for homes of distinction

This custom-built Magic Chef has the capacity and conveniences for homes with unusually large cooking requirements. Beautifully styled in satin finish stainless steel. This modern range has six top burners, two large ovens, plus a high level broiler and a generous size griddle. These and many other exclusive features are compactly built into this new Magic Chef. Engineered to use city, "Pyrofax" or other LP (bottled or tank) gases.

Send for descriptive literature . . . American Stove Company, 1641 S. Kingshighway Blvd., St. Louis 10, Mo.

© 1948, American Stove Company

● We don't know where to start telling you about all the automatic features and modern conveniences of this thrilling new Magic Chef. But let us make this suggestion: See it at your gas company or Magic Chef Dealer, compare it from every possible standpoint with any other range. When you've done this you'll know why more women cook on Magic Chef than on any other range.

AMERICAN STOVE COMPANY, DEPT. S-5, ST. LOUIS 2, MO.

YOU CAN COOK IT BETTER WITH *Magic Chef*

THE GAS RANGE WITH THE FAMOUS RED WHEEL

SEE IT AT YOUR GAS COMPANY OR MAGIC CHEF DEALER

All new G-E Thinline Air Conditioner takes up ⅓ less space!

G-E Thinline is ┊16 ½┊ inches "thin"... no unsightly overhang!

Why swelter when you can switch from hot, humid misery to cool, cool comfort with a G-E Thinline Room Air Conditioner!

HERE is a completely new concept in room air conditioners that offers top performance, yet actually takes up one-third less space than previous corresponding models.

It fits flush with your inside wall, yet has no unsightly overhang outside. And not only, does it offer you amazing cooling capacity and dehumidification—its High

Power Factor Design *assures economy of operation!*

You have a choice of many different comfort-conditions just at the flick of a finger. Delightfully cooled, filtered air pours quietly into your room, makes your days and nights comfortable all summer long! See your G-E dealer today for a demonstration —he's listed in your classified phone book.

General Electric Company, Room Air Conditioner Department. Appliance Park, Louisville 1, Kentucky.

Most models available in Canada.

Progress Is Our Most Important Product

GENERAL  ELECTRIC

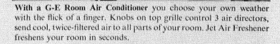

With a G-E Room Air Conditioner you choose your own weather with the flick of a finger. Knobs on top grille control 3 air directors, send cool, twice-filtered air to all parts of your room. Jet Air Freshener freshens your room in seconds.

Set it—and forget it! Accessory timer (slight additional cost) automatically turns unit on and off at any desired time for each of seven days. Ideal for offices and rooms used only part time.

Overcomes stale, unpleasant odors. Push a button; a jet of deodorizing spray mixes silently with the filtered air, freshens your whole room in seconds. Included in all models without cost.

IT'S FUN TO 'PHONE!

Turn a few minutes into fun by calling a friend or loved one. Whether it's
down the street, or across the country, a sunny get-together makes the day
a lot brighter. Lonely feelings are laughed away by a cheerful visit by telephone.
So treat yourself to a welcome break and just for fun—call someone!

BELL TELEPHONE SYSTEM

Since the telephone was "a toy"...

BACK in 1881, when this curious old switchboard was in use, many people thought of the telephone as little more than a toy. Apparatus was crude and service was limited—but even then the telephone was proving its worth.

As the Bell System took shape, Western Electric in 1882 became the System's manufacturing unit in order to assure a dependable source of dependable equipment. Through the years, we've made *good* equipment that serves long and faithfully with a minimum of upkeep—the kind that helps make possible dependable, low cost telephone service.

● For 68 years now, Western Electric people who *make* telephone equipment, Bell scientists who *design* it and Bell Telephone company people who *operate* it, have worked most closely together with a single purpose: to give you an ever-improving telephone service that is high in quality, low in cost.

A UNIT OF THE BELL SYSTEM SINCE 1882

WORLD'S FASTEST...

SILENT

Smith-Corona

...America's new Favorite in portables!

NEW! COLORSPEED KEYBOARD—Rimless, nonglare keys are "fingerprint-shaped" to cup your fingertips. Key-letterings can't wear off!

NEW! QUICKSET MARGINS—Simplest, easiest ever! Just depress Pointers and slide them along Paper Scale. And you can see the settings!

NEW! ACOUSTICAL VENTS—New, quieter operation! Typing noises are muffled by enclosed design and vented out rear of chassis!

★ It's the All-New Smith-Corona . . . and, whether you're six or sixty — expert or beginner — it's bound to be *your* favorite, too! You'll know what "World's Fastest" means, the minute you feel its new, "peppier" touch — its smooth, lightning-fast response . . . and there's less chance of jamming the keys than ever before! Has the easiest margin-set system ever offered on a portable . . . a new *Line Retainer* that "remembers" the writing level, if you release it to type between-lines . . . a new *Super-Speed Escapement* that lets the typebars print and snap back faster than on *any* other portable . . . plus full-size office typewriter keyboard, of course.

See your Smith-Corona Dealer *now* for a complete demonstration, prices and convenient payment terms!

The All-New Smith-Corona

L C SMITH & CORONA TYPEWRITERS INC SYRACUSE 1 N Y *Canadian factory and offices, Toronto, Ontario.*
Makers also of famous Smith-Corona Office Typewriters, Adding Machines, Vivid Duplicators, Ribbons and Carbons. © 1950

Pfft!
IT'S FILLED!

Sheaffer's *New Touch Down* Filler

Just touch-<u>down</u>...it's no trick! Just that simple—just that quick!
A single down-stroke and <u>air alone</u> does the work...empties...
cleans...refills your new Sheaffer's pen completely! Never before
has there been a pen like Sheaffer's Touchdown. See it—try it
at your Sheaffer dealer's.

W. A. Sheaffer Pen Co., Ft. Madison, Iowa, U.S.A. In Canada: Malton, Ont.

SHEAFFER'S
WHITE DOT ● OF DISTINCTION

One MORE Good Reason
why Sheaffer's is
America's First Choice

SENTINEL
Pen . . . $15.00
Other pieces $10.00 and $5.00
Ladies' Tuckaway Size, same price
Gift Packaged Free

NEW
Lady Sheaffer

'SKRIPSERT' FOUNTAIN PEN

never goes near an ink bottle!

Just unscrew the tip of your *Lady Sheaffer* pen, drop in a *Skripsert* cartridge of famous Sheaffer SKRIP writing fluid, and you're ready to write! Your fingers stay clean...and so does the point. A handy fabric pouch holds your reserve *Skripsert* supply —so you'll always be prepared.

always at hand when you need it!

Sheaffer puts an end to digging in your hand bag, looking for your pen! Each *Lady Sheaffer* pen rests in a harmonizing fabric Purse Case. Simply tuck...or clip it inside your carry-all, and there you are...always ready with your lovely *Lady Sheaffer* fountain pen!

a fine fountain pen...a fashion accessory!

Never before—a fountain pen so unique it actually becomes a distinctive accessory, expressing *your* personal taste in fine jewelry and fabrics! Sheaffer use enamel, silver and other precious metals for the look of luxurious jewelry...offering a delightful range of choice...to make this a pen you will be proud to hold. And because it's a superb Sheaffer fountain pen you'll love the way you write with i Smoothly, clearly *your* way of writing!

CAMPUS BOUND

19 exquisite models.
$10⁰⁰ to $110⁰⁰
(Patents Pending)

(Models shown are, from top down,
$12.50, $15.00*, $15.00, $10.00)

Available today in all better stores

*FEDERAL TAX INCLUDED

© 1958 W. A. SHEAFFER PEN COMPANY, FORT MADISON, IOWA

SHEAFFER'S

Seventeen—August, 1958

Seventeen, August 1958

45

To honor its 33,000,000th watch—
Waltham Watch Company Proudly Presents

the magnificent new

WALTHAM
series 33

The 33,000,000th Waltham Watch produced in America since 1850 was the inspiration for Waltham's magnificent _new_ "Series 33." Breath-taking in its beauty . . . superb in its craftsmanship . . . the _new_ Waltham "Series 33" is the finest Waltham of all time! From $33.75 to $1,000, including Federal Tax.

America's Traditional Gift Watch for almost 100 Years

NETTIE 17 Jewel $39.75   ALDEA 17 Jewel $65.00   CORDELIA 17 Jewel $55.00   MONA 17 Jl. 14 Kt. $71.50   ESSEX 17 Jewel $62.50   MELROSE 17 Jewel $39.75   ENSIGN 17 Jewel $49.50

THE NEW
Waltham SERIES 33
is America's Most Beautiful Watch

Brilliantly original and distinctive in design . . . with a streamlined slenderness you'd think impossible in watches of such matchless precision . . . the new Waltham "Series 33" is a masterpiece of the American watchmaker's art.

THE NEW
Waltham SERIES 33
is America's Most Beautifully-Balanced Watch

Every Waltham precision balance-wheel has 4 mean time screws of precious gold . . . a feature found only in the most costly chronographs. No Waltham ever has less than 17 jewels and 4 adjustments.

made in America
by American Craftsmen

Only watches made exclusively in America, by American precision craftsmen, can display this emblem. Look for it before you buy.

As with all precious gifts, let your jeweler be your trusted advisor. Waltham Watch Company, Waltham, Massachusetts © 1948.

Bausch & Lomb *Ray-Ban*® — the most distinguished name in sun glasses

AT LEADING OPTICAL AND QUALITY OUTLETS FROM $7.25 TO $24.95

Ray-Ban Sun Glasses take the strain out of driving. Comfortable, cool vision hour after hour. She's driving safely wearing the Ray-Ban "Stroller".

Ray-Ban Sun Glasses for sportsmen. Gradient Density lens has special coating for extra protection from overhead and reflected glare. Shown, Ray-Ban "Outdoorsman".

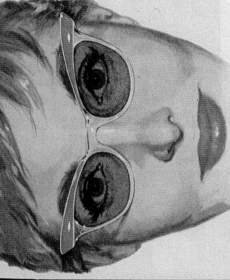

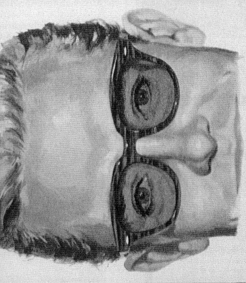

Ray-Ban Sun Glasses are fashion accessories. Colors to match your summer clothes, beachwear, or bathing suits. Illustrated is the Ray-Ban "Smart Set".

Ray-Ban lenses are precision ground — from finest Bausch & Lomb optical glass. Neutral gray G-15 lens, developed for the Air Force. Shown in new "Orion".

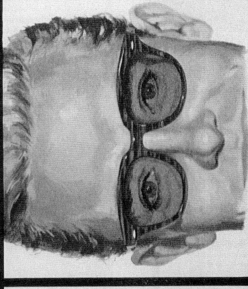

Ray-Ban Sun Glasses shut out cruel glare. Absorb ultra-violet and infra-red rays. Retard wrinkles and "crow's feet". She's wearing the Ray-Ban "Gadabout".

Ray-Ban Sun Glasses ... for sports fans everywhere. Have more fun, watching or playing. Shown is the aristocrat of sun glasses, the Ray-Ban "Signet".

WEAR GLASSES? Get a pair in your prescription with Ray-Ban Orthogon lenses, single vision or bifocals. Bausch & Lomb Optical Co., Rochester 2, N. Y.

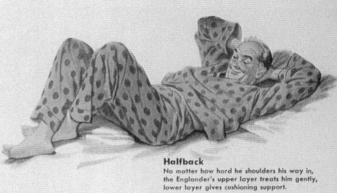

Busybody
Let her fuss and let her fidget all day. She'll still get sound, restful sleep on the responsive cradling of the Englander.

Halfback
No matter how hard he shoulders his way in, the Englander's upper layer treats him gently, lower layer gives cushioning support.

Englander
AMERICA'S MOST LUXURIOUS
mattress

never before
a mattress like this
COMPLETE COMFORT FOR EVERY KIND OF SLEEPER

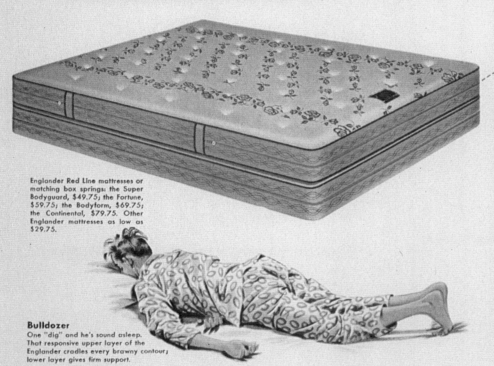

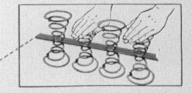

Englander Red Line mattresses or matching box springs: the Super Bodyguard, $49.75; the Fortune, $59.75; the Bodyform, $69.75; the Continental, $79.75. Other Englander mattresses as low as $29.75.

1. Upper layer fits your body
2. Lower layer fits your weight

Every sleeper needs *two* types of support for completely restful sleep. And now, for the first time, the Englander Red Line Mattress gives you this double layer of support.

In the diagram above, notice how the springs are joined *in the center* by a flexible ribbon of steel (not in the old-fashioned tied-top-or-bottom way or in cotton sacks). Every part of your body is restfully cushioned by the upper layer of springs, while the lower layer provides firm over-all support for your weight. No matter how you sleep or how much you weigh, you sleep better on an Englander.

See the Englander at fine furniture and department stores—the only mattress with the Red Line.

Bulldozer
One "dig" and he's sound asleep. That responsive upper layer of the Englander cradles every brawny contour; lower layer gives firm support.

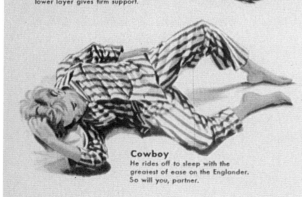

Mannequin
A pretty pose and sweet reposing too, with the Englander's two layers of support.

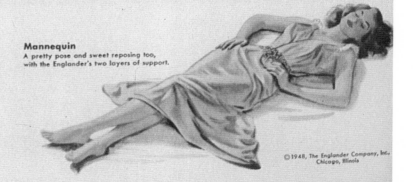

Cowboy
He rides off to sleep with the greatest of ease on the Englander. So will you, partner.

©1948, The Englander Company, Inc., Chicago, Illinois

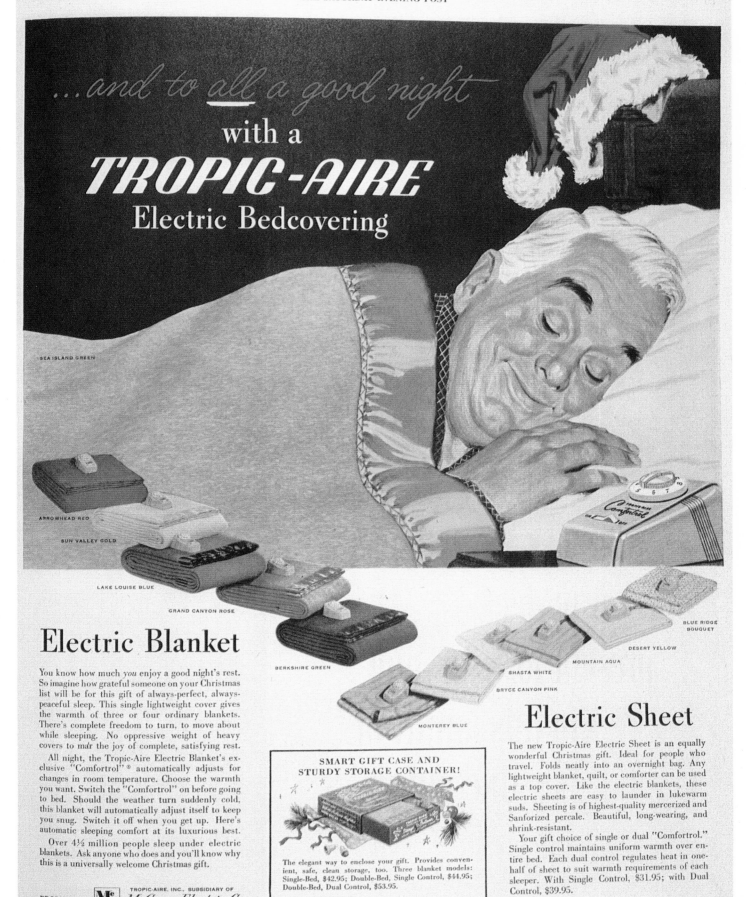

...and to all a good night—
with a
TROPIC-AIRE
Electric Bedcovering

SEA ISLAND GREEN

ARROWHEAD RED

SUN VALLEY GOLD

LAKE LOUISE BLUE

GRAND CANYON ROSE

BERKSHIRE GREEN

MONTEREY BLUE

BRYCE CANYON PINK

SHASTA WHITE

MOUNTAIN AQUA

DESERT YELLOW

BLUE RIDGE BOUQUET

Electric Blanket

You know how much *you* enjoy a good night's rest. So imagine how grateful someone on your Christmas list will be for this gift of always-perfect, always-peaceful sleep. This single lightweight cover gives the warmth of three or four ordinary blankets. There's complete freedom to turn, to move about while sleeping. No oppressive weight of heavy covers to mar the joy of complete, satisfying rest.

All night, the Tropic-Aire Electric Blanket's exclusive "Comfortrol"® automatically adjusts for changes in room temperature. Choose the warmth you want. Switch the "Comfortrol" on before going to bed. Should the weather turn suddenly cold, this blanket will automatically adjust itself to keep you snug. Switch it off when you get up. Here's automatic sleeping comfort at its luxurious best.

Over 4½ million people sleep under electric blankets. Ask anyone who does and you'll know why this is a universally welcome Christmas gift.

PRODUCTS OF **McGraw Electric Co.**
TROPIC-AIRE, INC., SUBSIDIARY OF
ELGIN, ILLINOIS. ©1953

SMART GIFT CASE AND STURDY STORAGE CONTAINER!

The elegant way to enclose your gift. Provides convenient, safe, clean storage, too. Three blanket models: Single-Bed, $42.95; Double-Bed, Single Control, $44.95; Double-Bed, Dual Control, $53.95.

Electric Sheet

The new Tropic-Aire Electric Sheet is an equally wonderful Christmas gift. Ideal for people who travel. Folds neatly into an overnight bag. Any lightweight blanket, quilt, or comforter can be used as a top cover. Like the electric blankets, these electric sheets are easy to launder in lukewarm suds. Sheeting is of highest-quality mercerized and Sanforized percale. Beautiful, long-wearing, and shrink-resistant.

Your gift choice of single or dual "Comfortrol." Single control maintains uniform warmth over entire bed. Each dual control regulates heat in one-half of sheet to suit warmth requirements of each sleeper. With Single Control, $31.95; with Dual Control, $39.95.

Saturday Evening Post, December 1953
49

Give me a 'Lucky' every time...

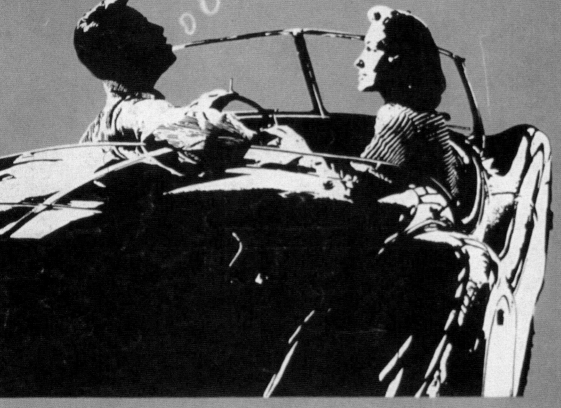

they're fresh from the U.S.A.

In the U.S.A., where Lucky Strike cigarettes are made, they are
packed in Reyseal aluminium wraps. Reyseal—resistant to moisture and
air—*seals in* all the natural flavor and aroma of the fine tobacco,
so that every cigarette comes to you as fresh as the day it was made.

Life, April 1950

Life, May 1948

Straight from the shoulder...
If you want a TREAT
instead of a TREATMENT
...smoke Old Golds

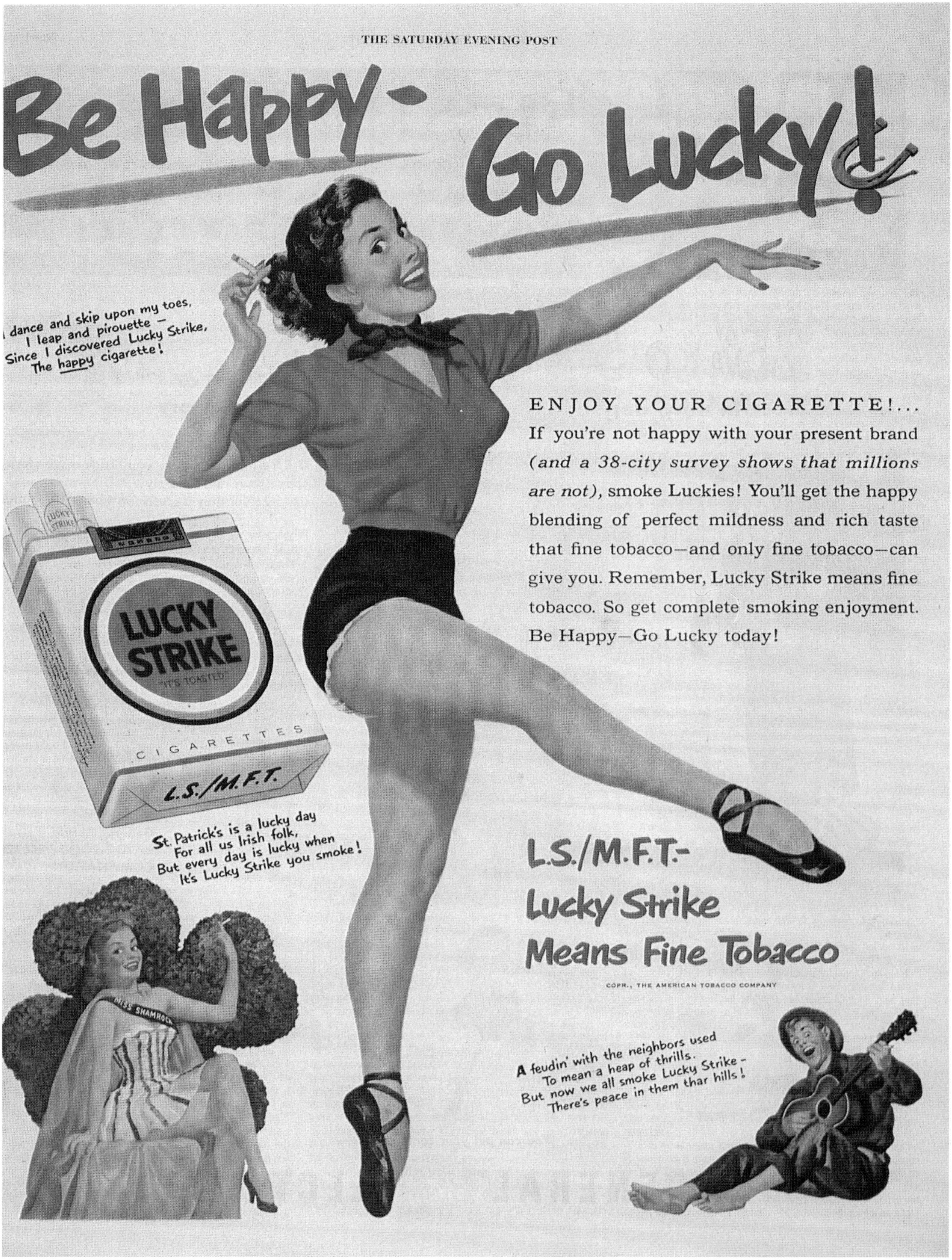

Saturday Evening Post, March 1951

LUCKIES TASTE BETTER!

Cleaner, Fresher, Smoother!

Nothing—no, nothing— beats better taste!

You know, yourself, you smoke for enjoyment. And you get enjoyment only from the *taste* of a cigarette.

Luckies taste better. You can even see why when you strip the paper from a Lucky by tearing down the seam.

You see that your Lucky remains a perfect cylinder of fine tobacco—long strands of fine, mild, good-tasting tobacco. Yes, L.S./M.F.T.—Lucky Strike *means* fine tobacco—in a cigarette that's made better to taste better.

So, for the thing you want most in a cigarette . . . for better taste . . .

Be Happy-GO LUCKY!

LUCKY STRIKE
"IT'S TOASTED"
CIGARETTES

PRODUCT OF *The American Tobacco Company*
AMERICA'S LEADING MANUFACTURER OF CIGARETTES

© A. T. Co.

Saturday Evening Post, July 1953

Saturday Evening Post, January 1956

Born gentle

Proud mothers, please forgive us if we too feel something of the pride of a new parent. For new Philip Morris, today's Philip Morris, is delighting smokers everywhere. Enjoy the gentle pleasure, the *fresh unfiltered flavor*, of this new cigarette, born gentle, then refined to special gentleness in the making. Ask for new Philip Morris in the smart new package.

©1956, Philip Morris Inc.

King Size
or
Regular
Snap-open
Pack

New Philip Morris...*gentle for modern taste*

ALL OVER AMERICA — SMOKERS ARE CHANGING TO CHESTERFIELD

AT THE *Paramount Pictures* CAFE CONTINENTAL

I certify that Chesterfield is our largest selling cigarette by 3 to 1

Pauline Kessinger MANAGER

DEAN MARTIN and JERRY LEWIS
"buy 'em by the carton"

See them starring in
"SAILOR BEWARE"
A Hal Wallis Production,
Paramount Release

3 to 1 because of
MILDNESS — plus
No Unpleasant After-taste*

* FROM THE REPORT OF A WELL-KNOWN RESEARCH ORGANIZATION

...AND ONLY CHESTERFIELD HAS IT!

Chesterfield
CIGARETTES
LIGGETT & MYERS TOBACCO CO.

CHESTERFIELD

Try them Today!

New Philip Morris "Snap-Open" Pack
opens in a jiffy ... closes tight to keep flavor in!

You get all the rich flavor and fine aroma of more *rare vintage tobacco*—King Size or Regular!

See for yourself what vintage tobacco means to *you* in taste, smoothness and enjoyment. Try PHILIP MORRIS, the cigarette that contains more rare vintage tobacco than other leading brands. And remember, you just...

ZIP *the tape* ... **SNAP** *it's open* ... **PRESTO** *it closes!*

What a convenient pack for America's *finest* cigarette!

CALL FOR PHILIP MORRIS KING SIZE or REGULAR

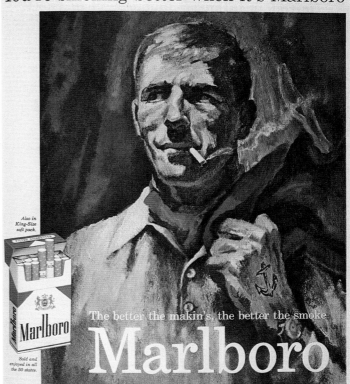

August 29, 1959

You're smoking better when it's Marlboro

Also in King-Size soft pack.

The better the makin's, the better the smoke

Marlboro

Sold and enjoyed in all the 50 states.

You get better makin's in a Marlboro. The exclusive Filter-Flavor Formula gives you flavor you can get hold of through a filter that does what it's there for. Try Marlboro for comfortable mildness.

Seek no more my lady! If you've been meditating over a specially smart Valentine for him, here's the answer... The El Producto Cigar Album. This handsome Album with its choice selection of cigars affords him the unique opportunity of enjoying five famous El Producto shapes and sizes... from sleek Panetela to distinguished Corona. Certainly a new and flattering way to a man's heart.

El Producto Cigar Album...25 fine quality cigars $3.75.

THE SATURDAY EVENING POST

♪♪ "Give Zippo for Christmas...one zip and it's lit. The gift for a lifetime...a sure-fire hit!"

"Zippo lights in a breeze With the greatest of ease!"

"It's guaranteed mechanically. Repairs are absolutely free!"

"Zippo's styled to combine Ruggedness with smart design!"

"Nothing is so prized As a Zippo personalized!"

"Give Zippo with pleasure— The gift people treasure!"

ZIPPO
one-zip windproof lighter

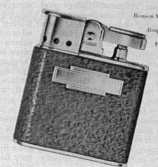

Ronson **WHIRLWIND**, windproof lighter, disappearing windshield. Genuine pigskin. $9.00. Other finishes, from $7.50

All for one—one for all! That's the Ronson story. For most smokers, no matter what their brand of smoke, prefer the World's *Finest Lighter* . . . Ronson, of course, with its famous one-finger, one-motion safety action: **"press...it's lit! release...it's out!** Safely out the instant you lift your finger."

Ronson **STANDARD**, engine turned design. $6.00. Other finishes, $6.50 to $7.50

RONSON lights them all...

world's greatest lighter ®

Illustrated are just three of the many handsome and efficient Pocket Ronsons. Your dealer has these and other smart Ronsons, precision-built to fine jewelry standards— for pocket and purse, $6 to $200; for table and desk, in heavy silver plate, from $8.50 (plus tax).

Ronson **ADONIS**, slim as a fine watch, tortoise enamel finish. $12.50. Other finishes, $10 to $200.

Tune in Ronson's "20 Questions" Saturday nights (Sunday nights Pacific Coast), Mutual Network and Ronson's "Johnny Desmond Show" Sunday nights (Monday nights Pacific Coast), Mutual Network. See and hear Ronson on Television, too.

RONSON. Newark, N.J. · Toronto, Ont. · London, Eng.

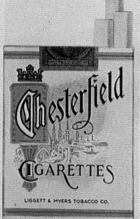

Saturday Evening Post, October 1949

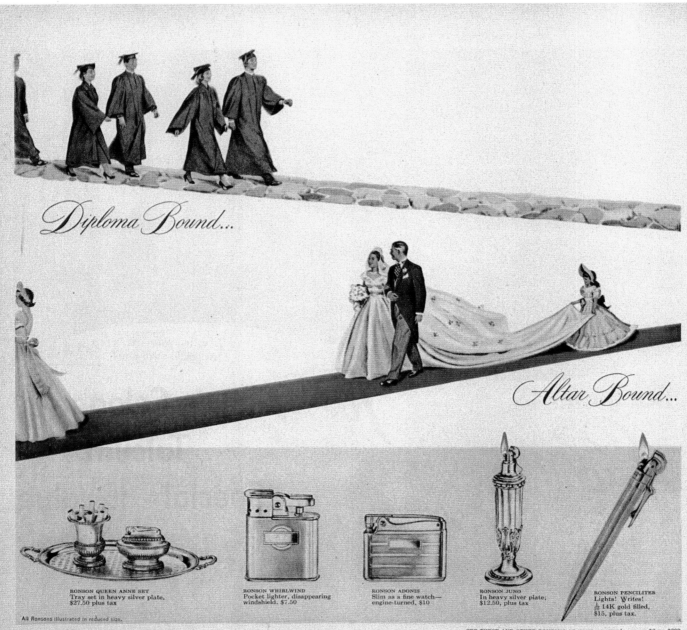

Diploma Bound...

Altar Bound...

RONSON QUEEN ANNE SET
Tray set in heavy silver plate,
$27.50 plus tax

All Ronsons illustrated in reduced sizes.

RONSON WHIRLWIND
Pocket lighter, disappearing
windshield. $7.50

RONSON ADONIS
Slim as a fine watch—
engine-turned, $10

RONSON JUNO
In heavy silver plate;
$12.50, plus tax

RONSON PENCILITER
Lights! Writes!
1/20 14K gold filled,
$15, plus tax

SEE THESE AND OTHER RONSONS AT YOUR DEALER'S, FROM $6 TO $200.

Everybody
loves a

RONSON ®

WORLD'S GREATEST LIGHTER

How MANY GIFTS are equally appropriate for the starry-eyed
graduate . . . the blushing bride . . . or her stammering groom?
And, as a matter of fact, for all the wedding attendants,
in memory of the great event?

Takes something pretty wonderful! Takes a Ronson!
In that large and varied selection you'll find the lighter
that's just exactly *right*.

But always look for the trademark RONSON. It tells *you*, and
everybody else that you're giving the *best*. Every Ronson is
precision-built to fine jewelry standards. Every Ronson faithfully
promises to honor and obey, for years of dependable lights.

Remember! All lighters work best
with Ronsonol Fuel and Ronson Redskin 'Flints'.

Enjoy Ronson's "20 Questions"! RADIO — Sat. nights (Sun. nights, Pacific Coast), MBS.
TELEVISION — Friday nights in many cities.

RONSON Newark, N. J. • Toronto, Ontario, Canada • London, Eng.

Press—it's lit!
Release—it's out!
Safely out the instant
you lift your finger

For modern people, modern taste...
Pepsi-Cola refreshes without filling

NEVER was a whole generation better to look at than the slim, lithe youngsters of today. What's more, insurance figures say they'll live longer than their grandparents did. And much of the reason is their modern, more sensible diet.

That's why today Pepsi-Cola is more popular than ever. Because it has constantly kept pace with the wholesome change in taste to lighter foods and lighter beverages.

Today's lighter Pepsi-Cola is dry, never too sweet or heavy, reduced in calories. It refreshes without filling.

Enjoy it whenever you want refreshment—either in the familiar big economy bottle for two, or in the new single-drink size. Have a Pepsi—the modern, the *light* refreshment.

PEPSI-COLA
The Light refreshment

Fashion is for the Slender

TODAY'S stylists are doing wonders for the looks of modern woman. But give some credit, too, to the woman herself. For the modern figure is her own creation.

Her greatest care and pride is to keep that figure young. Her taste, therefore, is for lighter foods and lighter beverages.

As good for her health as for her looks, this is the way of living that gives her the slender lines that fashion insists on, that men admire, that health authorities and insurance companies applaud.

This is the modern trend with which Pepsi-Cola, too, has steadily kept pace. That's why today's Pepsi is light, dry (not sweet), reduced in calories—and more popular than ever!

It is the modern, the light refreshment, made for modern taste. Pepsi-Cola refreshes without filling.

Enjoy it in the familiar economy bottle that serves two people, or in the smaller, single-drink size, just right for one. Have a Pepsi.

Pepsi-Cola refreshes without filling

Look, November 1953

Today's pace is for the

Slender

LITTLE Miss Sit-by-the-fire doesn't live there any more. Today, she's Miss Get-up-and-go—and never mind the weather!

For the up-to-date woman, conscious of her waistline, has set the trend to lighter, less filling food and drink. Her wholesome eating habits make her active, keep her slender.

Today's Pepsi-Cola, reduced in calories, goes right along with this modern taste in diet. Never heavy, never too sweet, Pepsi-Cola refreshes without filling.

Have a Pepsi—the modern, the *light* refreshment.

Pepsi-Cola

refreshes without filling

To Merry People everywhere

WE, who bring the *light* refreshment your way, wish you the most light-hearted of Holidays.

Pepsi-Cola
the *Light* refreshment

Christmas hat especially created by Sally Victor for Pepsi-Cola.

Saturday Evening Post, December 1958

Between pictures, say,

"Pepsi, please"

WHETHER you're at your favorite neighborhood theatre ... or a drive-in ... you'll agree today's modern people are feature attractions. Their trim, slender figures are the happy result of the modern trend toward lighter, less-filling food and drink.

Pepsi-Cola heartily supports this sensible diet plan. For today's Pepsi, reduced in calories, is never heavy, never too sweet. It's the modern, the *light* refreshment. Say "Pepsi, please"!

The **Light** refreshment

Saturday Evening Post, May 1958

66

OLD *Custom* **NEW** *Style*

Refresh without filling

NOTICE how the new-day woman won't sit still for the filling foods of yesteryear. She's thankful for the whole modern trend toward light food and drink. And don't you notice the slim-and-slender difference?

Pepsi-Cola has this same modern view about diet. Today's Pepsi-Cola, reduced in calories, is never heavy, never too sweet. Have a Pepsi. Refresh without filling.

Pepsi-Cola

the *Light* refreshment

Saturday Evening Post, April 1959

There's this about Coke . . .

"It couldn't be better"

How many times you've said,
"What I want is a Coke"—
meaning *just that!* Yes, Coca-Cola
has a place nothing else can fill.
Maybe it's the matchless flavor
. . . ever welcome, always delicious.
Or the feel of complete refreshment
after a pause with ice-cold Coke.
Whatever it is, it's made
Coke the most asked-for soft drink
in the world.

COKE" IS A REGISTERED TRADE-MARK.

COPYRIGHT 1954, THE COCA-COLA COMPANY

Under the sun of the Caribbees, talented Jack Potter
pictures a cheerful pause for Coca-Cola.

WHEREVER YOU CRUISE THE CARIBBEAN . . . when the moment comes
for Coca-Cola, here, too, you find it ready for you. In more than 100 countries of the
world today, the good taste that distinguishes Coca-Cola makes its enjoyment
a happy social custom. Have a Coke, best-loved sparkling drink in all the world.

SIGN OF GOOD TASTE

Refreshment . . . Real Refreshment

Looking pleasant is so easy at the soda fountain. There's good humor

and good company all around you. And, before you

is *the pause that refreshes* with ice-cold Coca-Cola. That's a lot

for 5 cents—a lot of real refreshment.

Ask for it either way . . . both trade-marks mean the same thing.

Saturday Evening Post, March 1958

"SEE YOU AT THE 'CHATTERBOX'

for COKE 'n' a snack!"

When the Big Man calls...that's the time to trot out your prettiest shirt and skirt. After all, many a prom "invite" has developed from an afternoon date! Then show him you're in the know by ordering refreshing Coca-Cola with your snack...makes every bite taste better! Chances are Coke, with its cheerful lift and real great taste, is his favorite drink, too. After all, Coke is the best-loved sparkling drink in all the world!

SIGN OF GOOD TASTE

So good in taste, in such good taste

Seventeen, August 1958

74

"THERE'll BE MISTLETOE AND MUSIC... a casserole and COKE"

Happy holiday party! And your clever centerpiece re-flects your knack for entertaining...it's a bowlful of colorful Christmas tree balls, one for every guest to take home when the party's over. For refreshments ...a well-seasoned casserole and a handsome container of ice-cold Coca-Cola! The great taste of Coke makes good food taste even better...and there's nothing like the cheerful lift of Coke to put everybody at their sparkling best!

Seventeen—December, 1958

"COKE" IS A REGISTERED TRADE-MARK. COPYRIGHT 1958 THE COCA-COLA COMPANY

SIGN OF GOOD TASTE

So good in taste, in such good taste

GOOD NEWS! Coke in big King Size, as well as Regular, now available in most parts of the U.S.A.

Seventeen, December 1958

75

THE WHITE ROCK GIRL *

* For over half a century — symbol of America's Finest beverages

White Rock

SPARKLING WATER
PALE DRY GINGER ALE

WHITE ROCK COLA · ORANGE · LEMON-LIME · RASPBERRY · ROOT BEER · SAZ-ROCK · CREAM SODA · TOM COLLINS MIXER

"Can't fool me. You're not Psyche!"

MAN: *Might* have made me think you were Psyche, if you hadn't just mentioned *ginger ale*. But Psyche is the symbol of White Rock—the *Sparkling Water*.

PSYCHE: Cross my *heart*, I'm Psyche, sir. The White Rock people now make a *whole line* of fine beverages. And when you try the tangier, tastier White Rock *Ginger Ale*—

MAN: Wish I could believe it, young lady. But, you see, I happen to be from Missouri.

PSYCHE: Fine! You'll be all the more delighted when you *do* become convinced. Here—look at this *label*. Why not try a glass right now?

MAN: "White Rock Ginger Ale" . . . And, *man*, —tastes like they really know how to make it, too! I misjudged you—*Psyche*. I'm sorry.

PSYCHE: I understand, sir. But you *couldn't* misjudge White Rock beverages. They're all of the same top quality that has kept White

Rock *Sparkling Water* famous ever since your grandfather first came over on the alkaline side.

*Psyche now symbolizes
a whole line of fine beverages*

White Rock Beverages

PUT MILES BETWEEN YOU AND THIRST WITH THIS
real thirst-quencher!

Nothing does it like Seven-Up

Dear Driver: Here's how to cover more miles than you thought you could between the "I'm thirsty-s". Just be sure your crew has 7-Up when you stop. This is the sparkling drink that really quenches. When you finish the last fresh-tasting sip, you feel no stickiness, no come-back thirst! (What better test for a quencher?) Ask your "map checker" to watch for the bright 7-Up signs all along your route! YOU LIKE IT...IT LIKES YOU

ADDS TO THE FUN FOR ALL!

"fresh up" with Seven-Up!

BE A "FRESH UP" FAMILY!

What a perfect way to spend a warm afternoon! The children enjoy the swing and the slide while Mom and Dad beam over their brood. And with sparkling 7-Up, chilled and inviting, it's an *extra happy* family occasion. Crystal-clear 7-Up, the *all-family* drink, has a "fresh up" goodness that adds a lot to family fun. It's so pure . . . so good . . . so completely wholesome, even toddling youngsters can "fresh up" with as much 7-Up as they want and just as often as they want. They just know 7-Up *likes them!* Be a "fresh up" family. Keep 7-Up chilled in your refrigerator. And enjoy this crystal-clear, *all-family* beverage as you work and play together. Buy a case of 7-Up today wherever you see those bright 7-Up signs.

7up
REG. U.S. PAT. OFF.

You like it . . . it likes you!

BUY A CASE TODAY!

Every Breakfast—a quick "toast 'n' coffee" or fried chicken and apple pie —should begin with Florida orange juice. It puts the *good* in "Good Morning," starts everyone off right.

It's always time for Florida Orange Juice...

your best daily source of the vitamin C you need every day

Take time out during a busy day and order a full, big glass of Florida orange juice for a quick pickup, lots of "go." Available almost everywhere—at fountains, restaurants, roadside stands.

Showtime—or any time family or friends get together serve Florida orange juice. The pleasant aid to sparkling good health—**with 3 to 5 times more vitamin C than non-citrus juices.**

Night Raiders can clean you out in a jiffy. So keep a big pitcher of Florida orange juice cold and handy. Make sure there's plenty of frozen or canned juice ready to open.

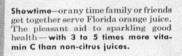

A full BIG glass

FLORIDA FROZEN Orange Concentrate

Your choice of Brand

FLORIDA ORANGE JUICE

Your choice of

Florida Citrus Commission, Lakeland, Florida

Costs about 4¢ a serving

Florida Fresh-Frozen Concentrate

Pure juice—no sugar added. Year-round source of the true flavor and vitamin C of fresh oranges. No fuss, no muss to fix. America's fastest growing family drink.

Florida Canned

Easy way to store and serve delicious Florida orange juice. Ready in seconds any time. Good-health-in-a-can —has up to 5 times the "C" of non-citrus juices.

Saturday Evening Post, June 1954

"... and she can have all the Canada Dry she wants"

Doctors . . . nurses . . . hospitals have been recommending Canada Dry Ginger Ale for years. They know, from professional experience, that Canada Dry has always been dry, wholesome, high in energy. For dryness—which means less sweet—is no new fad with Canada Dry. From the very beginning, it has been deliciously dry . . . less sweet . . . far more refreshing. That's what has made it the stand-by of three generations . . . one of the fastest-growing, best-liked beverages in the world. Enjoy some today . . . for a healthy change.

FOLLOW THE LEADER . . . YOU'LL GET THE BEST

Insist on "The Champagne of Ginger Ales"

Collier's, October 1954

COURVOISIER

COGNAC

The Brandy of Napoleon

Napoleon chose Courvoisier — and down through history Courvoisier has been the choice of those who could command the finest. It is the traditionally correct cognac — unchanging in quality—matchless in flavour and aroma.

* Courvoisier Cognac—and Courvoisier only—bears this registered phrase on every bottle. Reg. U. S. Pat. Off.

84 PROOF

Imported by W. A. TAYLOR & COMPANY, New York, N. Y. • Sole Distributors for the U. S. A.

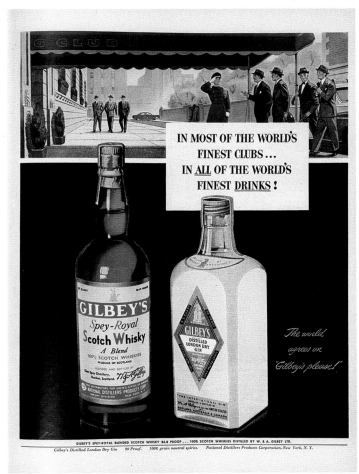

WILSON'S . . .

America's Finest

To Give...

WILSON'S CERTIFIED Ham COOK BEFORE EATING
Merry Christmas Happy New Year

WILSON'S *Tender Made* Ham READY TO EAT KEEP IN REFRIGERATOR

PREPARED BY SECRET PROCESS AND CONTROLLED TEMPERATURES

WILSON & CO., MANUFACTURER GENERAL OFFICE, CHICAGO, ILL.

WILSON & CO. INC

To Serve

Ham that bears the famous Wilson label has no equal for tenderness and flavor. Whether Wilson's Tender Made or Certified Smoked Ham is your choice · · · family and friends will cheer your good judgment.

See your favorite dealer. Choose your Wilson's holiday ham now.

Give a Wilson ham at Christmas time
Or serve one for good eating
A Tender Made or Certified
Is the season's favorite greeting

The Wilson label protects your table

Saturday Evening Post, November 1949

94

2 LBS.
FRESH-PICKED PEAS
in every can

If you bought these peas for quantity alone, they'd be a good buy—all shelled and ready to use. But you don't. You buy Green Giant Brand because you know no prettier peas ever popped out of a pod. Gathered dewy-fresh at the fleeting moment of perfect flavor. Washed in cool, soft water. Tested for tenderness. And sealed in Green Giant Brand cans within three short hours from their green-growing vines. *That's value!*

Listen to the Fred Waring Show on NBC every Saturday morning.

GREEN GIANT PEAS
BRAND

LOOK FOR THE
JOLLY GREEN GIANT
ON THE LABEL

17-oz. Can

GREEN GIANT
GREAT BIG
TENDER
SWEET PEAS

Minnesota Valley Canning Company, headquarters, Le Sueur, Minnesota; Fine Foods of Canada, Ltd., Tecumseh, Ontario. Also packers of Niblets Brand whole kernel corn.
"Green Giant" and "Niblets" Brands Reg. U. S. Pat. Off.

Sweet Dreams

The candy with the hole   only 5¢

Saturday Evening Post, February 1950

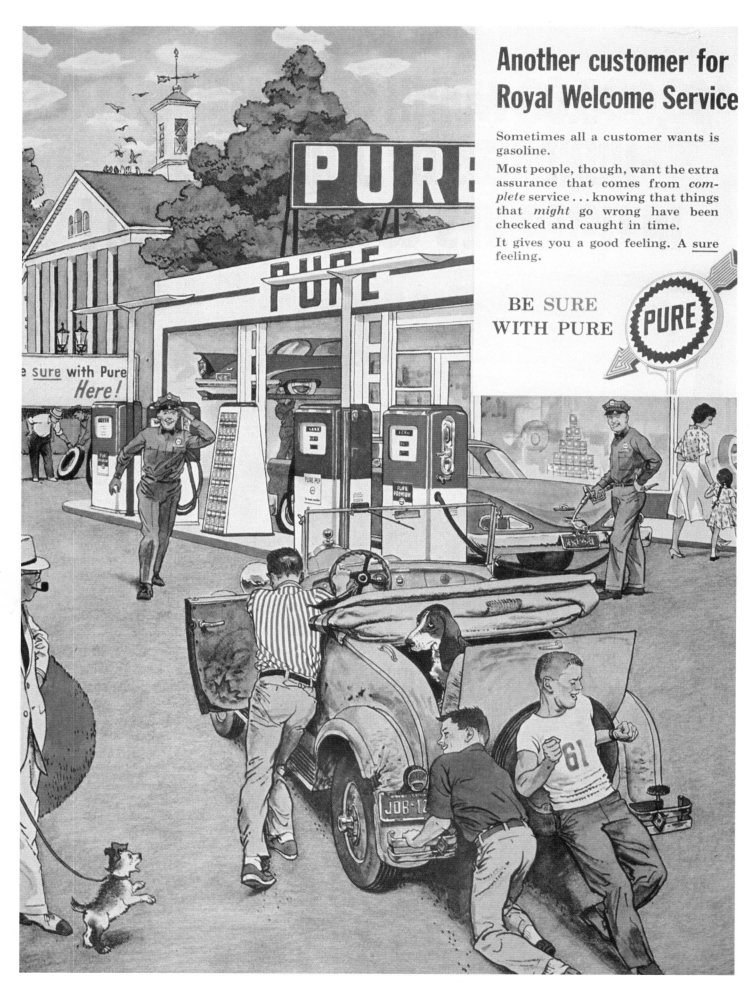

Another customer for Royal Welcome Service

Sometimes all a customer wants is gasoline.

Most people, though, want the extra assurance that comes from *complete* service ... knowing that things that *might* go wrong have been checked and caught in time.

It gives you a good feeling. A <u>sure</u> feeling.

BE SURE
WITH PURE **PURE**

THE SATURDAY EVENING POST

★ Golden State, Southern Pacific-Rock Island streamliner, Chicago to Los Angeles via El Paso, Tucson, Phoenix, Palm Springs.

Come to Arizona and California

...on the swift Golden State

★ **GOLDEN STATE** is the *only* streamliner direct to Tucson, Phoenix and Palm Springs. It starts you on this wonderful Great Circle Tour of the West, which you can combine with your next Arizona-California trip.

From Chicago take our swift *Golden State*—"smoothest streamliner to the Pacific Coast"—via El Paso (where you stopover for Carlsbad Caverns National Park if you wish), Douglas, Bisbee, Tucson and Phoenix. Basically in Arizona's famed desert resort country. Then Palm Springs and Los Angeles, San Diego, Old Mexico.

From Los Angeles, go North on our scenic *California Daylight* streamliner via Santa Barbara—470 miles of lovely Pacific surf, valley and mountain—to San Francisco. See the Golden Gate.

Then home via Reno, Ogden, Omaha and Chicago on our

luxurious *City of San Francisco*—"fastest thing on wheels between the Golden Gate and Chicago".

Or go North from San Francisco on our new *Shasta Daylight* streamliner, past 14,161-foot Mt. Shasta, through beautiful Oregon to Portland, thence home by the U.S. or Canadian line of your choice.

If you prefer, go home via New Orleans. From Arizona or Los Angeles take our fast *Sunset Limited* to El Paso, Texas resort country, San Antonio, Houston, New Orleans. (All-Diesel now, the *Sunset* will be a completely new, 42-hour streamliner later this year.)

Only Southern Pacific brings you to California one way, returns you another. You *see twice as much* on an S.P. Western trip. The two photo folders explain fully. Send for them today.

➤➤➤

SOUTHERN PACIFIC'S FOUR SCENIC ROUTES
SHOWING THE GOLDEN STATE ROUTE IN RED

SOUTHERN PACIFIC, Dept. SE-11
310 So. Michigan Avenue, Chicago 4, Illinois.
Please send me, free, the photo folders, "Your Vacation in Arizona" and "How to See Twice as Much on Your Trip to California".

NAME _____
ADDRESS _____
CITY _____ STATE _____
(If school student, state grade)

S·P The friendly Southern Pacific

THE SATURDAY EVENING POST

Even if they catch us, Willoughby...

YOU ONLY PAY ONCE ON THE RAILROADS!

Let's say it again, you only *pay once* for services rendered by the railroads. Yes, for either fare or freight you pay only one established rate.

But what's so extraordinary about that? Why should you pay more than once for any transportation service? As a matter of good business you shouldn't—as a matter of fact, you do. Here's just what happens. Other forms of transportation use highways, airports and waterways built and maintained largely by the people's tax money. So, you *pay twice* for using them—first in direct charges and *again* in your share of taxes necessary to build and keep up the public facilities used.

The railroads, on the other hand, build and maintain *their*

own steel highways, their own stations, bridges and tunnels. Not one red cent of your tax money is used to support them.

The railroads pay their own way, in every way.

Yet, in peace and in the emergency of war, it's the railroads we all depend upon, to deliver everything from guns to green vegetables. Truly, the railroad is *Mr. Transportation*.

The railroads want no special favors. They do want fair play, competition on an even-Steven basis. They are entitled to it and so are you. With open, "no-favorites" competition in the best American tradition, the railroads will serve you—and all the people—better than ever before.

Fair Play for America's Railroads

AMERICAN RAILWAY CAR INSTITUTE

Only Greyhound gives you all these travel features...

at great big savings!

Time-Saving Business Trips
You can save hours on many trips—because of Greyhound's high-frequency schedules and straight-through service. Cover more ground—and relax while you do it—traveling by Greyhound!

Your Choice of Scenic Routes
Almost all of America's natural wonders and beauty spots are best reached by highway... best seen from Greyhound Super-Coaches, which follow the Nation's most famous highways.

Amazing America Tours
They're fascinating! They're fun! They cost less! Greyhound Expense-Paid Tours of *This Amazing America* are complete vacations or shorter pleasure trips—planned in advance, by experts.

Express and Limited Schedules
To get you there faster, Greyhound provides Express and Limited schedules over many routes, direct to major cities or resort areas. Luxury at lowest cost!

Nationwide Coverage
A single Greyhound ticket can take you up, down, across, or completely around this Country—into Canada or Mexico! Greyhound alone serves all 48 States.

Charter Coaches for Your Group
From doorstep to doorstep, a Chartered Greyhound will keep your congenial crowd together on any excursion, to convention, sports event, or other attraction.

There's just one transportation system that can offer you *all* the important travel features illustrated on this page... and that's Greyhound! It's a fact that Greyhound gives you ultra-frequent, convenient schedules to all parts of America—at surprisingly low fares. But only Greyhound can provide all these *extra* features (and others, too)... proving itself just about the most complete and well-rounded travel service in the Land! Look over these advantages—and remember then the next time you plan a trip for yourself, your family, your club, or special group. And whenever you spend your good money for trips anywhere, make certain you get the best features of modern travel, *going Greyhound!*

Extra-Big Savings on Round-Trip Fares!
Everyone knows that Greyhound fares are amazingly low—but do you realize that Greyhound round-trip rates offer especially big savings—as much as 20 to 40 percent of the return cost of your trip—sometimes more?

Easychair Comfort
Slide into a soft-cushioned Greyhound easychair... and relax! SuperCoaches are tops in smooth-riding comfort—thousands of them are fully air-conditioned.

FREE! ILLUSTRATED FULL-COLOR MAP
"GAY DAYS AROUND AMERICA"
Mail this coupon to AMERICA CELEBRATES, Box 821, Chicago 90, Ill., for this very attractive wall-size map and information travel folder.

NAME _____
ADDRESS _____
CITY _____ STATE _____

GREYHOUND

A LOT MORE TRAVEL for A LOT LESS MONEY

BEACH DECKS SURROUND THE LARGE OUTDOOR TILED POOLS ON GRACE LINE "SANTAS"

Really relax on a GRACE LINE CRUISE
to the CARIBBEAN and SOUTH AMERICA

The "Santa Rosa" and "Santa Paula," especially designed for tropical cruising, provide every comfort and luxury: large outdoor tiled swimming pools; light, airy dining rooms on top decks; excellent cuisine; gracious public rooms; beauty salons; sun decks; attractive cocktail lounges; dance orchestras; shipboard entertainment and interesting trips ashore. Every room is outside, each with private bath. **Twelve Day Cruises from New York every Friday.** Also 16-18 Day Cruises every Friday from New York on cargo-passenger "Santas." See your travel agent or

GRACE LINE

10 Hanover Sq., New York, Agents and offices in all principal cities.

OVER THE RIVERS AND OVER THE WOODS

🎵 *to Grandmother's house we go* 🎵

There's a new road now to an old tradition. It's the TWA *high* way home
for Thanksgiving. And what a blessing it is to families separated
by too many rivers and too many woods . . . and *so* many years!
If you've let distance and lack of time keep *you* away too long, try traveling
this high way. Find out how TWA can make it very *near* to someone dear
—for even an *ocean* apart is only hours apart . . . by Skyliner!

*Where in the world do you want to go? For informa-
tion and reservations, call TWA or see your travel agent.*

ACROSS THE U.S. AND OVERSEAS . . . YOU CAN DEPEND ON TWA

TRANS WORLD AIRLINES

U.S.A. · EUROPE · AFRICA · ASIA

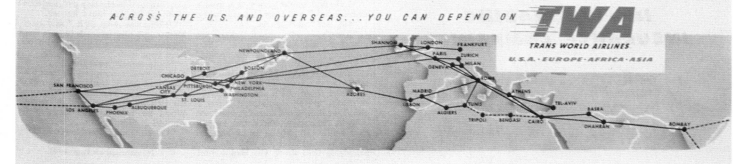

"ザ・フィフティーズ"

主な出来事

（1950～1959）

1950年

アメリカ

- リズ・テーラーがコンラッド・ヒルトン・ジュニアとはじめての結婚
- ボストンで現金280万ドル強奪事件
- 落下傘スカートが大流行

**"ザ・フィフティーズ"
主な出来事
(1950〜1959)**

世界

- 朝鮮戦争はじまる

日本

- 警察予備隊(自衛隊の前身)創設
- 金閣寺が放火で焼失
- 「チャタレー夫人の恋人」発禁

1951年

- 全米に赤狩りのマッカーシー旋風
- テレビ全米放送開始
- 人気スター・ナンバー・ワンは、ディーン・マーチン、ジェリー・ルイスのお笑いコンビ

- イラン石油国有化法を公布

- マッカーサー連合軍指令官が解任さる
- 「羅生門」がベニス映画祭でグランプリ受賞

1952年

- 米大統領にアイゼンハワー元師
- ゲーリー・クーパーがアカデミー最優秀男優賞受賞
- ３Ｄ映画が大ヒット

- 初の水爆実験
- 朝鮮休戦協定調印

- 日航木星号が三原山に墜落
- 白井義男が世界フライ級チャンピオン
- ＮＨＫテレビ放送開始

1953年

- 「アイ・ラブ・ルーシー」が全米テレビ番組のベストワンに選ばれる
- アカデミー最優秀女優賞はオードリー・ヘップバーン
- バーミューダ・パンツが男性に流行

- 英エリザベス女王戴冠式
- スターリン死去
- 英のヒラリーがエベレスト登頂に成功

- ジャズコンサート黄金期
- 伊東絹子がミス・ユニバース第3位

1954年

- 米最高裁、公立学校での人種隔離は違憲との判決
- マリリン・モンローがジョー・ディマジオと結婚
- グレース・ケリーにアカデミー女優賞
- アーネスト・ヘミングウェイにノーベル文学賞

- ディエンビエンフーが陥落、インドシナ休戦
- ソ連、原子力発電を開始

- マリリン・モンロー夫妻が来日
- 自衛隊が発足
- 青函連絡船洞爺丸が沈没
- 電気洗濯機の普及本格化

1955年

- ジェームス・ディーンが自動車事故で急死。
- ロサンゼルス郊外にディズニー・ランドがオープン
- デイビー・クロケット・ハットが流行

- 第1回ジュネーブ・サミット開かる（米、英、仏、ソ）
- ワルシャワ条約機構が成立

- 日本経済、復興から発展へ。神武景気
- マンボとチャチャチャが流行
- 映画「エデンの東」が大ヒット

1956年

- エルビス・プレスリーがスター・ダムへ
- グレース・ケリーがモナコのレーニエ大公と結婚
- アカデミー最優秀女優賞はイングリッド・バーグマン

- ハンガリー事件
- スエズ動乱
- ポーランドで反ソ暴動

- 売春防止法成立
- 日本、国連に加盟
- 東海道本線の全線電化
- 日本、ソ連と国交回復へ

*1957*年

- ・ブロードウェイのミュージカル
「ウェスト・サイド・ストーリー」がヒット
- ・バッグ・ドレスが流行

- ・ソ連が人工衛星スプートニク1号を打ち上げ

- ・東海村に原子炉第1号が完成
- ・南極に昭和基地

1958年　1959年

1958年

- 米、人工衛星「エクスプローラ」打ち上げに成功
- 全米でフラフープが大流行
- スーザン・ヘイワードがアカデミー最優秀女優賞を受賞

- 欧州経済協同体（ECC）が発足

- 日劇第1回ウェスタンカーニバル。ロカビリー・ブーム
- 1万円札発行
- 皇太子妃に正田美智子さんが決定

1959年

- アラスカ、ハワイが州に昇格。50州になる
- ロック・ハドソン、ドリス・デイ共演の「ピロー・トーク」が大ヒット
- パット・ブーンがゴールド・レコードを獲得
- 大学生のあいだで電話ボックス詰込みゲームが流行

- キューバ革命
- 中ソ対立が激化

- 皇太子ご成婚をきっかけにテレビの普及本格化。全国にミッチー・ブーム
- 安保反対デモ激化
- 伊勢湾台風で死者5200人

生田保年（いくた・やすとし）

1931年福岡市生まれ。應応義塾大学卒業。

東京新聞政治部、博報堂国際局勤務ののち、独立。

現在、共同プラニングセンター代表。市場調査、PR企画の仕事を通じて、海外の自動車市場や広告事情に詳しい。

著書に「アメリカン・カー・グラフィティ」「ビジネスジョーク"Now"」などがある。なお「アメリカン・カー・グラフィティ」の英語版が1987年秋、米国クロニクル・ブックスから出版されることになっている。

雑誌広告にみるアメリカングラフィティ

ザ・フィフティーズ 3

バラエティ

1987年7月25日　初版第1刷発行
1996年3月25日　初版第3刷発行

著者─────生田保年（いくた やすとし）©
発行者────久世利郎

印刷─────錦明印刷株式会社
製本─────錦明印刷株式会社
写植─────三和写真工芸株式会社

発行所────株式会社グラフィック社
　　　　　　〒102 東京都千代田区九段北1-9-12
　　　　　　☎03(3263)4318　振替・00130-6-114345

ISBN4-7661-0438-2 C3071